Comn
to Captivate

Dale Harbison Carnegie was an American writer and the developer of famous courses in self-development, salesmanship, corporate training, public speaking, and interpersonal skills. He is the author of the bestselling *How to Win Friends and Influence People*, *How to Stop Worrying and Start Living*, and many more self-help books.

Communicate to Captivate

Guide to *Persuasive Engagement*

Dale Carnegie

RUPA

Published by
Rupa Publications India Pvt. Ltd 2024
7/16, Ansari Road, Daryaganj
New Delhi 110002

Sales centres:
Bengaluru Chennai
Hyderabad Jaipur Kathmandu
Kolkata Mumbai Prayagraj

Edition copyright © Rupa Publications India Pvt. Ltd 2024

All rights reserved.
No part of this publication may be reproduced, transmitted,
or stored in a retrieval system, in any form or by any means,
electronic, mechanical, photocopying, recording or otherwise, without
the prior permission of the publisher.

P-ISBN:978-93-5702-990-2
E-ISBN:978-93-5702-898-1

Second impression 2024

10 9 8 7 6 5 4 3 2

Printed in India

This book is sold subject to the condition that it shall not, by way of
trade or otherwise, be lent, resold, hired out, or otherwise circulated,
without the publisher's prior consent, in any form of binding or
cover other than that in which it is published.

CONTENTS

1. Making Conversation Effective — 7
2. Earning the Right to Talk — 13
3. Essential Elements of Successful Speaking — 23
4. Develop Confidence — 30
5. The Voice — 43
6. Efficiency through Change of Pitch — 49
7. How to Open a Talk — 54
8. Speak Effectively, the Quick and Easy Way — 63
9. Expressing Genuine Interest in Others — 74
10. Concentration in Delivery — 85
11. Methods of Delivery — 89
12. The Power of Enthusiasm — 94
13. Growing a Vocabulary — 104
14. Talk about Your Own Mistakes First — 110
15. How Famous Speakers Prepared Their Addresses — 116
16. How to Make Your Meaning Clear — 121
17. Right Thinking and Personality — 127
18. The Talk to Convince — 133

19. Influencing by Persuasion   145
20. How to Criticize—and Not Be Hated for It   150
21. How to Close a Talk   155
22. Starting to Communicate   169

1

MAKING CONVERSATION EFFECTIVE

"It's much easier to become interested in others than it is to convince them to be interested in you."

The father of W.E. Gladstone considered conversation to be both an art and an accomplishment. Around the dinner table in his home, some topic of local or national interest, or some debated question was constantly being discussed. In this way a friendly rivalry for supremacy in conversation arose among the family, and an incident observed in the street, an idea gleaned from a book, a deduction from personal experience, was carefully stored as material for the family exchange. Thus his early years of practice in elegant conversation prepared the younger Gladstone for his career as a leader and speaker.

There is a sense in which the ability to converse effectively is efficient public speaking, for our conversation is often heard by many, and occasionally decisions of great moment hinge upon the tone and quality of what we say in private.

Indeed, conversation in the aggregate probably wields more power than press and platform combined. Socrates taught his great truths, not from public rostrums, but in personal converse. Men made pilgrimages to Goethe's library and Coleridge's home to be charmed and instructed by their speech, and the culture of many nations was immeasurably influenced by the thoughts that streamed out from those rich well-springs.

Most of the world-moving speeches are made in the course of conversation. Conferences of diplomats, business-getting arguments, decisions by boards of directors, considerations of corporate policy, all of which influence the political, mercantile and economic maps of the world, are usually the results of careful though informal conversation, and the man whose opinions weigh in such crises is he who has first carefully pondered the words of both antagonist and protagonist.

However important it may be to attain self-control in light social converse, or about the family table, it is undeniably vital to have oneself perfectly in hand while taking part in a momentous conference. Then the hints that we have given on poise, alertness, precision of word, clearness of statement, and force of utterance, with respect to public speech, are equally applicable to conversation.

The form of nervous egotism—for it is both—that suddenly ends in flusters just when the vital words need to be uttered, is the sign of coming defeat, for a conversation is often a contest. If you feel this tendency embarrassing you, be sure to listen to Holmes's advice:

'And when you stick on conversational burs, Don't strew your pathway with those dreadful urs.'

Here bring your will into action, for your trouble is a wandering attention. You must force your mind to persist along the chosen line of conversation and resolutely refuse to be diverted by any subject or happening that may unexpectedly pop up to distract you. To fail here is to lose effectiveness utterly.

Concentration is the keynote of conversational charm and efficiency. The haphazard habit of expression that uses bird-shot when a bullet is needed insures missing the game, for diplomacy of all sorts rests upon the precise application of precise words, particularly—if one may paraphrase Tallyrand—in those crises when language is no longer used to conceal thought.

WIN OVER YOUR WEAKNESSES

We may frequently gain new light on old subjects by looking at word-derivations. Conversation signifies in the original a turn-about exchange of ideas, yet most people seem to regard it as a monologue. Bronson Alcott used to say that many could argue, but few converse. The first thing to remember in conversation, then, is that listening—respectful, sympathetic, alert listening—is not only due to our fellow converser but due to ourselves. Many a reply loses its point because the speaker is so much interested in what he is about to say that it is really no reply at all but merely an irritating and humiliating irrelevancy.

Self-expression is exhilarating. This explains the eternal impulse to decorate totem poles and paint pictures, write poetry and expound philosophy. One of the chief delights of conversation is the opportunity it affords for self-expression. A good conversationalist who monopolizes all the conversation, will be voted a bore because he denies others the enjoyment of self-expression, while a mediocre talker who listens interestedly may be considered a good conversationalist because he permits his companions to please themselves through self-expression. They are praised who please: they please who listen well.

The first step in remedying habits of confusion in manner, awkward bearing, vagueness in thought, and lack of precision in utterance, is to recognize your faults. If you are serenely unconscious of them, no one—least of all yourself—can help you. But once diagnose your own weaknesses, and you can overcome them by doing four things:

1. WILL to overcome them, and keep on willing.
2. Hold yourself in hand by assuring yourself that you know precisely what you ought to say. If you cannot do that, be quiet until you are clear on this vital point.
3. Having thus assured yourself, cast out the fear of those who listen to you—they are only human and will respect your words if you really have something to say and say it briefly, simply, and clearly.
4. Have the courage to study the English language until you are master of at least its simpler forms.

CONVERSATIONAL HINTS

Choose some subject that will prove of general interest to the whole group. Do not explain the mechanism of a gas engine at an afternoon tea or the culture of hollyhocks at a stag party.

It is not considered good taste for a man to bare his arm in public and show scars or deformities. It is equally bad form for him to flaunt his own woes, or the deformity of someone else's character. The public demands plays and stories that end happily. All the world is seeking happiness. They cannot long be interested in your ills and troubles. George Cohan made himself a millionaire before he was thirty by writing cheerful plays. One of his rules is generally applicable to conversation: 'Always leave them laughing when you say good bye.'

Dynamite the 'I' out of your conversation. Not one man in nine hundred and seven can talk about himself without being a bore. The man who can perform that feat can achieve marvels without talking about himself, so the eternal 'I' is not permissible even in his talk.

If you habitually build your conversation around your own interests it may prove very tiresome to your listener. He may be thinking of bird dogs or dry fly fishing while you are discussing the fourth dimension, or the merits of a cucumber lotion. The charming conversationalist is prepared to talk in terms of his listener's interest. If his listener spends his spare time investigating Guernsey cattle or agitating social reforms, the discriminating conversationalist shapes his remarks accordingly. Richard Washburn Child says he knows a man of mediocre ability who can charm men much abler than himself when he discusses electric lighting. This same man probably would bore, and be bored, if he were forced to converse about music or Madagascar.

Avoid platitudes and hackneyed phrases. If you meet a friend from Keokuk on State Street or on Pike's Peak, it is not necessary to observe: 'How small this world is after all!' This observation was doubtless made prior to the formation of Pike's Peak. 'This old world is getting better every day.' 'Fanner's wives do not have to work as hard as formerly.' 'It is not so much the high cost of living as the cost of high living.' Such observations as these excite about the same degree of admiration as is drawn out by the appearance of a 1903-model touring car. If you have nothing fresh or interesting you can always remain silent. How would you like to read a newspaper that flashed out in bold headlines 'Nice Weather We Are Having,' or daily gave columns to the same old material you had been reading week after week?

> **Points to Remember**
>
> 1. Concentration is the primary criterion for effective and impressive conversations.
> 2. Self-diagnose your weaknesses and work on them instead of feeling sad about yourself.
> 3. To gain others' interest, stop talking about what troubles you. Talk about what troubles everyone.

2

EARNING THE RIGHT TO TALK

"An effective speaker knows that the success or failure of his talk is not for him to decide—it will be decided in the minds and hearts of his hearers."

Many years ago, a Doctor of Philosophy and a rough-and-ready fellow who had spent his youth in the British Navy were enrolled in one of our classes in New York. The man with the degree was a college professor; the ex-tar was the proprietor of a small side-street trucking business. His talks were far better received by the class than those given by the professor. Why? The college man used beautiful English. He was urbane, cultured, refined. His talks were always logical and clear. But they lacked one essential—concreteness. They were vague and general. Not once did he illustrate a point with anything approaching a personal experience. His talks were usually nothing more than a series of abstract ideas held together by a thin string of logic.

On the other hand, the trucking firm proprietor's language was definite, concrete, and picturesque. He talked in terms of everyday facts. He gave us one point and then backed it up by telling us what happened to him in the course of his business. He described the people he had to deal with and the headaches of keeping up with regulations. The virility and freshness of his phraseology made his talks highly instructive and entertaining.

I cite this instance, not because it is typical of college professors or of men in the trucking business, but because it illustrates the attention-compelling power of rich, colorful details in a talk.

There are four ways to develop speech material that guarantees audience attention. If you follow these four steps in your preparation you will be well on the way to commanding the eager attention of your listeners.

FIRST: LIMIT YOUR SUBJECT

Once you have selected your topic, the first step is to stake out the area you want to cover and stay strictly within those limits. Don't make the mistake of trying to cover the open range. One young man attempted to speak for two minutes on the subject of "Athens from 500 B.C. to the Korean War." How utterly futile! He barely had gone beyond the founding of the city before he had to sit down, another victim of the compulsion to cover too much in one talk. This is an extreme example, I know; I have heard thousands of talks, less encompassing in scope, that failed to hold attention for the same reason—they covered far too many points. Why? Because it is impossible for the mind to attend to a monotonous series of factual points. If your talk sounds like the World Almanac you will not be able to hold attention very long. Take a simple subject, like a trip to Yellowstone Park. In their eagerness to leave nothing out, most people have something to say about every scenic view in the Park. The audience is whisked from one point to another with dizzying speed. At the end, all that remains in the mind is a blur of waterfalls, mountains, and geysers. How much more memorable such a talk would be if the speaker limited himself to one aspect of the Park, the wildlife or the hot springs, for example. Then there would be time to develop the kind of pictorial detail that would make Yellowstone Park come alive in all its vivid color and variety.

This is true of any subject, whether it be salesmanship, baking cakes, tax exemptions, or ballistic missiles. You must limit and select before you begin, narrow your subject down to an area that will fit the time at your disposal.

In a short talk, less than five minutes in duration, all you can expect is to get one or two main points across. In a longer talk, up to thirty minutes, few speakers ever succeed if they try to cover more than four or five main ideas.

SECOND: DEVELOP RESERVE POWER

It is far easier to give a talk that skims over the surface than to dig down for facts. But when you take the easy way you make little or no impression on the audience. After you have narrowed your subject, then the next step is to ask yourself questions that will deepen your understanding and prepare you to talk with authority on the topic you have chosen: "Why do I believe this? When did I ever see this point exemplified in real life? What precisely am I trying to prove? Exactly how did it happen?"

Questions like these call for answers that will give you reserve power, the power that makes people sit up and take notice. It was said of Luther Burbank, the botanical wizard, that he produced a million plant specimens to find one or two superlative ones. It is the same with a talk. Assemble a hundred thoughts around your theme, then discard ninety.

"I always try to get ten times as much information as I

use, sometimes a hundred times as much," said John Gunther not long ago. The author of the bestselling "Inside" books was speaking of the way he prepared to write a book or give a talk.

On one occasion in particular, his actions bore out his words. In 1956, he was working on a series of articles on mental hospitals. He visited institutions, talked to supervisors, attendants, and patients. A friend of mine was with him, giving some small assistance in the research, and he told me they must have walked countless miles upstairs and down, along corridors, building to building, day after day. Mr. Gunther filled notebooks. Back in his office, he stacked up government and state reports, private hospital reports, and reams of committees' statistics.

"In the end," my friend told me, "he wrote four short articles, simple enough and anecdotal enough to make good speeches. The paper on which they were typed weighed, perhaps, a few ounces. The filled notebooks, and everything else he used as the basis for the few ounces of product, must have weighed twenty pounds."

Mr. Gunther knew that he was working with pay dirt He knew he couldn't overlook any of it. An old hand at this sort of thing, he put his mind to it, and he sifted out the gold nuggets.

A surgeon friend of mine said: "I can teach you in ten minutes how to take out an appendix. But it will take me four years to teach you what to do if something goes wrong." So it is with speaking: Always prepare so that you are ready for any emergency, such as a change of emphasis because of a previous speaker's remarks, or a well-aimed question from the audience in the discussion period following your talk.

You, too, can acquire reserve power by selecting your topic as soon as possible. Don't put it off until a day or two before you have to speak. If you decide on the topic early you will have the inestimable advantage of having your subconscious mind working for you. At odd moments of the day when you are free from your work, you can explore your subject, refine the ideas you want to convey to your audience. Time ordinarily spent in reverie while you are driving home, waiting for a bus, or riding the subway, can be devoted to mulling over the subject matter of your talk. It is during this incubation period that flashes of insight will come, just because you have determined your topic far in advance and your mind subconsciously works over it.

Norman Thomas, a superb speaker who has commanded the respectful attention of audiences quite opposed to his political point of view, said: "If a speech is to be of any importance at all, the speaker should live with the theme or message, turning it over and over in his mind. He will be surprised at how many useful illustrations or ways of putting his case will come to him as he walks the street, or reads a newspaper, or gets ready for bed, or wakes up in the morning. Mediocre speaking very often is merely the inevitable and the appropriate reflection of mediocre thinking, and the consequence of imperfect acquaintance with the subject in hand."

While you are involved in this process you will be under strong temptation to write your talk out, word for word. Try not to do this, for once you have set a pattern, you are likely to be satisfied with it, and you may cease to give it any more constructive thought. In addition, there is the danger of memorizing the script. Mark Twain had this to say about such memorization: "Written things are not for speech; their form is literary; they are stiff, inflexible, and will not lend themselves to happy effective delivery with the tongue. Where their purpose is merely to entertain, not to instruct, they have to be limbered up, broken up, colloquialized, and turned into the common form of unpremeditated talk; otherwise they will bore the house—not entertain it."

Charles F. Kettering, whose inventive genius sparked the growth of General Motors, was one of America's most renowned and heartwarming speakers. Asked if he ever wrote out any part or all of his talks, he replied: "What I have to say is, I believe, far too important to write down on paper. I prefer to write on my audience's mind, on their emotions, with every ounce of my being. A piece of paper cannot stand between me and those I want to impress."

THIRD: FILL YOUR TALK WITH ILLUSTRATIONS AND EXAMPLES

In the *Art of Readable Writing,* Rudolf Flesch begins one of his chapters with this sentence: "Only stories are really readable." He then shows how this principle is used by *Time* and *Reader's Digest.* Almost every article in these top-circulation magazines either is written as pure narrative or is generously sprinkled with anecdotes. There is no denying the power of a story to hold attention in talking before groups as well as writing for magazines.

Norman Vincent Peale, whose sermons have been heard by millions on radio and television, says that his favorite form of supporting material in a talk is the illustration or example. He once told an interviewer from the *Quarterly Journal of Speech* that "the true example is the finest method I know of to make an idea clear, interesting, and persuasive. Usually, I use several examples to support each major point."

Readers of my books are soon aware of my use of the anecdote as a means of developing the main points of my message. The rules from *How to Win Friends and Influence People* can be listed on one and a half pages. The other two hundred and thirty pages of the book are filled with stories and illustrations to point up how others have used these rules with wholesome effect.

FOURTH: USE CONCRETE, FAMILIAR WORDS THAT CREATE PICTURES

In the process of getting and holding attention, which is the first purpose of every speaker, there is one aid, one technique, that is of the highest importance. Yet, it is all but ignored. The average speaker does not seem to be aware of its existence. He has probably never consciously thought about it at all. I refer to the process of using words that create pictures. The speaker who is easy to listen to is the one who sets images floating before your eyes. The one who employs foggy, commonplace, colorless symbols sets the audience to nodding.

Pictures, Pictures. Pictures. They are as free as the air you breathe. Sprinkle them through your talks, your conversation, and you will be more entertaining, more influential.

Herbert Spencer, in his famous essay on the "Philosophy of Style," pointed out long ago the superiority of terms that call forth bright pictures:

"We do not think in generals but in particulars... We should avoid such a sentence as:

"'In proportion as the manners, customs, and amusements of a nation are cruel and barbarous, the regulations of their penal code will be severe!'

"And in place of it, we should write:

"'In proportion as men delight in battles, bull fights, and combats of gladiators, will they punish by hanging, burning, and the rack.'"

Picture-building phrases swarm through the pages of the

Bible and through Shakespeare like bees around a cider mill. For example, a commonplace writer would have said that a certain thing would be "superfluous," like trying to improve the perfect. How did Shakespeare express the same thought? With a picture phrase that is immortal: "To gild refined gold, to paint the lily, to throw perfume on the violet."

Did you ever pause to observe that the proverbs that are passed on from generation to generation are almost all visual sayings? "A bird in the hand is worth two in the bush." "It never rains but it pours." "You can lead a horse to water but you can't make him drink." And you will find the same picture element in almost all the similes that have lived for centuries and grown hoary with too much use: "Sly as a fox." "Dead as a doornail." "Flat as a pancake." "Hard as a rock."

Lincoln continually talked in visual terminology. When he became annoyed with the long, complicated, red-tape reports that came to his desk in the White House, he objected to them, not with colorless phraseology, but with a picture phrase that it is almost impossible to forget. "When I send a man to buy a horse," he said, "I don't want to be told how many hairs the horse has in his tail. I wish only to know his points."

Make your eye appeals definite and specific. Paint mental pictures that stand out as sharp and clear as a stag's antlers silhouetted against the setting sun. For example, the word "dog" calls up a more or less definite picture of such an animal—perhaps a cocker spaniel, a Scottish terrier, a St. Bernard, or a Pomeranian. Notice how much more distinct an image springs into your mind when a speaker says "bulldog"—the term is less inclusive. Doesn't "a brindle bulldog" call up a still more explicit picture? Is it not more vivid to say "a black Shetland pony" than to talk of "a horse"? Doesn't "a white bantam rooster with a broken leg" give a much more definite and sharp picture than merely the word "fowl"?

In *The Elements of Style,* William Strunk, Jr., states: "If those who have studied the art of writing are in accord on any one point, it is on this: the surest way to arouse and hold the attention of the reader is by being specific, definite, and concrete. The greatest writers—Homer, Dante, Shakespeare—are effective largely because they deal in particulars and report the details that matter. Their words call up pictures." This is as true of speaking as of writing.

I once devoted a session years ago in my course in Effective Speaking to an experiment in being factual. We adopted a rule that in every sentence the speaker must put either a fact or a proper noun, a figure, or a date. The results were revolutionary. The class members made a game of catching one another on generalities; it wasn't long before they were talking, not the cloudy language that floats over the head of an audience, but the clear-cut, vigorous language of the man on the street.

"An abstract style," said the French philosopher Alain, "is always bad. Your sentences should be full of stones, metals, chairs, tables, animals, men, and women."

This is true of everyday conversation as well. In fact, all that has been said in this chapter about the use of detail in talks before groups applies to general conversation. It is detail that makes conversation sparkle. Anyone who is intent upon making himself a more effective conversationalist may profit by following the advice contained in this chapter. Salesmen, too, will discover the magic of detail when applied to their sales presentations. Those in executive positions, housewives, and teachers will find that giving instructions and dispensing information will be greatly improved by the use of concrete, factual detail.

> **Points to Remember**
>
> 1. Instead of covering every point, stick to a few points and concisely explain them.
> 2. It's better to speak in anecdotal form to gain effectiveness and rapt attention.
> 3. Don't be abstract. It is boring.

3

ESSENTIAL ELEMENTS OF SUCCESSFUL SPEAKING

*"Tell the audience what you're going
to say, say it; then tell them what you've said."*

When we start to learn any new thing, like French, or golf, or public speaking, we never advance steadily. We do not improve gradually. We do it by sudden jerks, by abrupt starts. Then we remain stationary a time, or we may even slip back and lose some of the ground we have previously gained. These periods of stagnation, or retrogression, are well known by all psychologists; and they have been named "plateaus in the curve of learning". Students of public speaking will sometimes be stalled for weeks on one of these plateaus. Work as hard as they may, they cannot get off it. The weak ones give up in despair. Those with grit persist, and they find that suddenly, overnight, without their knowing how or why it has happened, they have made great progress. They have lifted from the plateau like an aeroplane. Abruptly they have found the knack of the thing. Abruptly they have acquired naturalness and force and confidence in their speaking.

You may always, as we have noted elsewhere in these pages, experience some fleeting fear, some shock, some nervous anxiety the first few moments you face an audience. John Bright felt it to the end of his busy career; so did Gladstone; so did Bishop Wilberforce; so did a score of other eminent speakers. Even the greatest of the musicians have felt it in spite of their innumerable public appearances. Paderewski always fidgeted nervously with his cuffs immediately before he sat down at the piano. Nordica felt her heart racing. So did Sembrich. So did Emma Eames. But it vanished quickly, all of this audience fear, like a mist in the August sunshine.

Their experience will be yours. If you will but persevere, you will soon eradicate everything but this initial fear; and that will be initial fear, and nothing more. After the first few sentences, you will have control of yourself. You will be speaking with positive pleasure.

DON'T GIVE UP

One time a young man who aspired to study law, wrote to Lincoln for advice, and Lincoln replied: "If you are resolutely determined to make a lawyer of yourself, the thing is more than half done already... Always bear in mind that your own resolution to succeed is more important than any other one thing."

Lincoln knew. He had gone through it all. He had never, in his entire life, had more than a total of one year's schooling. And books? Lincoln once said he had walked and borrowed every book within fifty miles of his home. A log fire was usually kept going all night in the cabin. Sometimes he read by the light of that fire. There were cracks between the logs, and Lincoln often kept a book sticking in a crack. As soon as it was light enough to read in the morning, he rolled over on his bed of leaves, rubbed his eyes, pulled out the book and began devouring it.

He walked twenty and thirty miles to hear a speaker and, returning home, he practiced his talks everywhere—in the fields, in the woods, before the crowds gathered at Jones' grocery at Gentryville. He joined literary and debating societies in New Salem and Springfield, and practiced speaking on the topics of the day much as you are doing now as a member of this course.

A sense of inferiority always troubled him. In the presence of women he was shy and dumb. When he courted Mary Todd he used to sit in the parlour, bashful and silent, unable to find words, listening while she did the talking. Yet that was the man who, by practice and home study, made himself into the speaker who debated with the accomplished orator, Senator Douglas. That was the man who, at Gettysburg, and again in his second inaugural address, rose to heights of eloquence that have rarely been attained in all the annals of mankind.

Small wonder that, in view of his own terrific handicaps and pitiful struggle, he wrote: "If you are resolutely determined to make a lawyer of yourself, the thing is more than half done already."

There is an excellent picture of Abraham Lincoln in the President's office. "Often when I had some matter to decide," said Theodore Roosevelt, "something involved and difficult to dispose of, something where there were conflicting rights and interests, I would look up at Lincoln, try to imagine him in *my* place, try to figure out what he would do in the same circumstances. It may sound odd to you, but, frankly, it seemed to make my troubles easier of solution."

Why not try Roosevelt's plan? Why not, if you are discouraged and feeling like giving up the fight to make a speaker of yourself, why not pull out of your pocket one of the five dollar notes that bear a likeness of Lincoln, and ask yourself what he would do under the circumstances. You know what he would do. You know what he did do. After he had been beaten by Stephen A. Douglas in the race for the US Senate, he admonished his followers not to "give up after one nor one hundred defeats".

THE CERTAINTY OF REWARD

How I wish I could get you to prop this book open on your breakfast table every morning for a week until you had memorized these words from Professor William James, the famous psychologist:

> Let no youth have any anxiety about the upshot of his education, whatever the line of it may be. If he keeps faithfully busy each hour of the working day, he may safely leave the final result to itself. He can, with perfect certainty, count on waking up some fine morning to find himself one of the competent ones of his generation, in whatever pursuit he may have singled out.

And now, with the renowned Professor James to fall back upon, I shall go so far as to say that if you pursue this course faithfully and with enthusiasm, and keep right on practicing intelligently, you may confidently hope to wake up one fine morning and find yourself one of the competent speakers of your city or community.

Regardless of how fantastic that may sound to you now, *it is true as a general principle*. Exceptions, of course, there are. A man with an inferior mentality and personality, and with nothing to talk about, is not going to develop into a local Daniel Webster, but, *within reason*, the assertion is correct.

The entire question of your success as a speaker hinges upon only two things—your native ability, and the depth and strength of your desires.

I have known and carefully watched literally thousands of men trying to gain self-confidence and the ability to talk in public. Those that succeeded were, in only a few instances, men of unusual brilliancy. For the most part, they were the ordinary run of businessmen that you will find in your own hometown. But they kept on. Smarter men sometimes got discouraged or too deeply immersed in money making, and they did not get very far, but the ordinary individual with grit and singleness of purpose—at the end of the chapter, he was at the top.

That is only human and natural. Don't you see the same thing occurring all the time in commerce and the professions? Rockefeller said some time ago that the first essential for success in business was patience. It is likewise one of the first essentials for success in this course.

Marshal Foch led to victory by far the greatest army the world has ever seen, and he declared that he had only one virtue: never despairing.

When the French had retreated to the Marne in 1914, General Joffre instructed the generals under him, in charge of two million men, to stop retreating and begin an offensive. This new battle, one of the most decisive in the world's history, had raged for two days when General Foch, in command of Joffre's centre, sent him one of the most impressive messages in military records: "My centre gives way. My right recedes. The situation is excellent. I shall attack."

That attack saved Paris.

So, my dear speaker, when the fight seems hardest and most hopeless, when your centre gives way and your right recedes, "the situation is excellent". Attack! Attack! Attack, and you will save the best part of your manhood—your courage and faith.

CLIMBING THE "WILDER KAISER"

A few summers ago, I started out to scale a peak in the Austrian Alps called the Wilder Kaiser. Baedeker said that the ascent was difficult, and a guide was essential for amateur climbers. We, a friend and I, had none, and we were certainly amateurs, so a third party asked us if we thought we were going to succeed. "Of course," we replied.

"What makes you think so?" he inquired.

"Others have done it without guides," I said, "so I know it is within reason, and *I never undertake anything thinking defeat.*"

As an Alpinist, I am the merest, bungling novice, but that is the proper psychology for anything from essaying public speaking to an assault on Mount Everest.

Think success in this course. See yourself in your imagination talking in public with perfect self-control.

It is easily in your power to do this. Believe that you will succeed. Believe it firmly and you will then do what is necessary to bring success about.

The most valuable thing that most members acquire from a course in public speaking is an increased confidence in themselves, an additional faith in their ability to achieve. And than that, what is more important for one's success in almost any undertaking?

THE WILL TO WIN

Here is a bit of sage advice from Elbert Hubbard that I cannot refrain from quoting. If the average man would only apply and live the wisdom contained in it, he would be happier, more prosperous:

Whenever you go out of doors, draw the chin in, carry the crown of the head high and fill the lungs to the utmost; drink in the sunshine, greet your friends with a smile and put soul into every handclasp. Do not fear being misunderstood and do not waste a minute thinking about your enemies. Try to fix firmly in your mind what you would like to do, and then, without veering off direction, you will move straight to the goal. Keep your mind on the great and splendid things you would like to do, and then, as the days go gliding by, you will find yourself unconsciously seizing upon the opportunities that are required for the fulfilment of your desire, just as the coral insect takes from the running tide the elements it needs. Picture in your mind the able, earnest, useful person you desire to be, and the thought you hold is hourly transforming you into that particular individual… Thought is supreme. Preserve a right mental attitude—the attitude of courage, frankness and good cheer. To think rightly is to create. All things come through desire and every sincere prayer is answered. We become like that on which our hearts are fixed. Carry your chin in and the crown of your head high. We are gods in the chrysalis.

Points to Remember

1. Whether you fail once or a hundred times, do not give up.
2. Consistent efforts eventually bear fruit.
3. Believe in the power of manifestation.

4

DEVELOP CONFIDENCE

"There are always three speeches, for every one you actually gave. The one you practiced, the one you gave, and the one you wish you gave."

GET THE FACTS ABOUT FEAR OF SPEAKING IN PUBLIC

You are not unique in your fear of speaking in public. Surveys in colleges indicate that eighty to ninety per cent of all students enrolled in speech classes suffer from stage fright at the beginning of the course. I am inclined to believe that the figure is higher among adults at the start of my course, almost one hundred per cent.

A certain amount of stage fright is useful! It is nature's way of preparing us to meet unusual challenges in our environment. So, when you notice your pulse beating faster and your respiration speeding up, don't become alarmed. Your body, ever alert to external stimuli, is getting ready to go into action. If these physiological preparations are held within limits, you will be capable of thinking faster, talking more fluently, and generally speaking with greater intensity than under normal circumstances.

Many professional speakers have assured me that they never completely lose all stage fright. It is almost always present just before they speak, and it may persist through the first few sentences of their talk. This is the price these men and women pay for being like race horses and not like draft horses. Speakers who say they are "cool as a cucumber" at all times are usually as thick-skinned as a cucumber and about as inspiring as a cucumber.

The chief cause of your fear of public speaking is simply that you are unaccustomed to speak in public. For most people, public speaking is an unknown quantity, and consequently one fraught with anxiety and fear factors. For the beginner, it is a complex series of strange situations, more involved than, say, learning to play tennis or drive a car. To make this fearful situation simple and easy: practice, practice, practice. You will find, as thousands upon thousands have, that public speaking can be made a joy instead of an agony merely by getting a record of successful speaking experiences behind you.

The story of how Albert Edward Wiggam, the prominent lecturer and popular psychologist, overcame his fear, has been an inspiration to me ever since I first read it. He tells how terror-struck he was at the thought of standing up in high school and delivering a five-minute declamation.

"As the day approached," he writes, "I became positively ill Whenever the dreadful thought occurred to me, my whole head would flush with blood and my cheeks would burn so painfully that I would go out behind the school building and press them against the cold brick wall to try to reduce their surging blushes. It was the same way with me in college.

"On one occasion, I carefully memorized a declamation beginning, 'Adam and Jefferson are no more.' When I faced the audience, my head was swimming so I scarcely knew where I was. I managed to gasp out the opening sentence, stating that 'Adams and Jefferson have passed away.' I couldn't say another word, so I bowed…and walked solemnly back to my seat amid great applause. The president got up and said, 'Well, Edward, we are shocked to hear the sad news, but we will do our best to bear up under the circumstances.' During the uproarious laughter that followed, death would surely have been a welcome relief. I was ill for days afterward.

"Certainly the last thing on earth I ever expected to become was a public speaker."

A year after he left college, Albert Wiggam was in Denver. The political campaign of 1896 was raging over the issue of Free Silver. One day he read a pamphlet explaining the proposals of the Free Silverites; he became so incensed over what he considered the errors and hollow promises of Bryan and his followers, that he pawned his watch for enough money to get back to his native Indiana. Once there, he offered his services to speak on the subject of sound money. Many of his old school friends were in the audience. "As I began," he writes, "the picture of my Adams and Jefferson speech in college swept over me. I choked and stammered and all seemed to be lost. But, as Chauncey Depew often said, both the audience and I managed somehow to live through the introduction; and encouraged by even this tiny success, I went on talking for what I thought was about fifteen minutes. To my amazement, I discovered I had been talking an hour and a half!

"As a result, within the next few years, I was the most surprised person in the world to find myself making my living as a professional public speaker.

"I knew at first hand what William James meant by the habit of success."

Yes, Albert Edward Wiggam learned that one of the surest

ways of overcoming the devastating fear of speaking before groups is to get a record of successful experiences behind you.

You should expect a certain amount of fear as a natural adjunct of your desire to speak in public, and you should learn to depend on a limited amount of stage fright to help make you give a better talk.

If stage fright gets out of hand and seriously curtails your effectiveness by causing mental blocks, lack of fluency, uncontrollable tics, and excessive muscular spasm, you should not despair. These symptoms are not unusual in beginners. If you make the effort, you will find the degree of stage fright soon reduced to the point where it will prove a help and not a hindrance.

PREPARE IN THE PROPER WAY

The principal speaker at a New York Rotary Club luncheon several years ago was a prominent government official. We were looking forward to hearing him describe the activities of his department.

It was obvious almost at once that he had not planned his speech. At first he tried to talk impromptu. Failing in that attempt, he pulled out of his pocket a sheaf of notes which evidently had no more order than a flatcar full of scrap iron. He fumbled awhile with these, all the time becoming more embarrassed and inept in his delivery. Minute by minute he became more helpless, more bewildered. But he kept on floundering, apologizing, trying to make some semblance of sense out of his notes and raising a glass of water with a trembling hand to his parched lips. He was a sad picture of a man completely overcome by fright, due to almost total lack of preparation. He finally sat down, one of the most humiliated speakers I have ever seen. He made his talk as Rousseau says a love letter should be written: he began without knowing what he was going to say, and finished without knowing what he had said.

Since 1912, it has been my professional duty to evaluate over five thousand talks a year. From that experience, one great lesson stands out like Mount Everest, towering above all the others: *only the prepared speaker deserves to be confident.* How can anyone ever hope to storm the fortress of fear if he goes into battle with defective weapons, or with no ammunition at all? "I believe," said Lincoln, "that I shall never be old enough to speak without embarrassment when I have nothing to say."

If you want to develop confidence, why not do the one thing that will give you security as a speaker? "Perfect love," wrote the Apostle John, "casteth out fear." So does perfect preparation. Daniel Webster said he would as soon think of appearing before an audience half-clothed as half-prepared.

Never memorize word for word: By "perfect preparation" do I mean that you should memorize your talk? To this question I give back a thunderous NO. In their attempts to protect their egos from the dangers of drawing a mental blank before an audience, many speakers fall headlong into the trap of memorization. Once a victim of this type of mental dope addiction, the speaker is hopelessly bound to a time-consuming method of preparation that destroys effectiveness on the platform.

When H. V. Kaltenborn, the dean of American news commentators, was a student at Harvard University, he took part in a speech contest. He selected a short story entitled "Gentlemen, the King." He memorized it word for word and rehearsed it hundreds of times. The day of the contest he announced the title, "Gentlemen, the King." Then his mind went blank. It not only went blank; it went black. He was terrified. In desperation he started telling the story in his own words. He was the most surprised boy in the hall when the judges gave him first prize. From that day to this, H. V. Kaltenborn has never read nor memorized a speech. That has been the secret of success in his broadcasting career. He makes a few notes and talks naturally to his listeners without a script.

The man who writes out and memorizes his talks is wasting his time and energy, and courting disaster. All our lives we have been speaking spontaneously. We haven't been thinking of words. We have been thinking of ideas. If our ideas are clear, the words come as naturally and unconsciously as the air we breathe.

Even Winston Churchill had to learn that lesson the hard way. As a young man, Churchill wrote out and memorized his speeches. Then one day, while delivering a memorized talk before the British Parliament, he stopped dead in his mental tracks. His mind went blank. He was embarrassed, humiliated! He began his last sentence all over again. Again his mind went blank and his face scarlet He sat down. From that day to this, Winston Churchill has never attempted to deliver a memorized talk.

If we memorize our talk word for word, we will probably forget it when we face our listeners. Even if we do not forget our memorized talk, we will probably deliver it in a mechanical way. Why? Because it will not come from our hearts, but from our memories. When talking with people privately, we always think of something we want to say, and then we go ahead and say it without thinking of words. We have been doing that all our lives. Why attempt to change it now? If we do write out and memorize our talks, we may have the same experience that Vance Bushnell had.

Vance was a graduate of the Beaux Arts School in Paris,

and later became vice-president of one of the largest insurance companies in the world—the Equitable Life Assurance Society. Years ago, he was asked to address a conference of two thousand Equitable Life representatives from all over America at a meeting in White Sulphur Springs, West Virginia. At that time, he had been in the life insurance business for only two years, but he had been highly successful, so he was scheduled to make a twenty-minute talk.

Vance was delighted to do so. He felt it would give him prestige. But, unfortunately, he wrote out and memorized his talk. He rehearsed forty times in front of a mirror. He had everything down pat: every phrase, every gesture, every facial expression. It was flawless, he thought.

However, when he stood up to deliver his address, he was terrified. He said: "My part in this program is…" His mind went blank. In his confusion, he took two steps backward and tried to start all over again. Again, his mind went blank. Again he took two steps back and tried to start. He repeated this performance three times. The platform was four feet high; there was no railing at the back; and there was a space five feet wide between the back of the platform and the wall. So, the fourth time he stepped back, he toppled backwards off the platform and disappeared into space. The audience howled with laughter. One man fell off his chair and rolled in the aisle. Never before nor since in the history of the Equitable Life Assurance Society has anyone ever given such a comic performance. The astonishing part of the story is that the audience thought it was really an act. The old-timers of the Equitable Life are still talking about his performance.

But what about the speaker, Vance Bushnell? Vance Bushnell himself told me it was the most embarrassing occasion of his life. He felt so disgraced that he wrote out his resignation.

Vance Bushnell's superiors persuaded him to tear up his resignation. They restored his self-confidence; and Vance Bushnell, in later years, became one of the most effective speakers in his organization. But he never memorized a talk again. Let us profit by his experience.

I have heard countless scores of men and women try to deliver memorized talks, but I don't remember even one speaker who wouldn't have been more alive, more effective, more human, if he had tossed his memorized talk into the waste basket. If he had done that, he might have forgotten some of his points. He might have rambled, but at least he would have been human.

Abe Lincoln once said: "I don't like to hear a cut-and-dried sermon. When I hear a man preach, I like to see him act as if he were fighting bees." Lincoln said he wanted to hear a speaker cut loose and get excited. No speaker ever acts as if he were fighting bees when he is trying to recall memorized words.

Assemble and Arrange Your Ideas Beforehand: What, then, is the proper method of preparing a talk? Simply this: search your background for significant experiences that have taught you something about life, and assemble *your* thoughts, *your* ideas, *your* convictions, that have welled up from these experiences. True preparation means brooding over your topics. As Dr. Charles Reynold Brown said some years ago in a memorable series of lectures at Yale University: "Brood over your topic until it becomes mellow and expansive...then put all these ideas down in writing, just a few words, enough to fix the idea... put them down on scraps of paper—you will find it easier to arrange and organize these loose bits when you come to set your material in order." This doesn't sound like such a difficult program, does it? It isn't. It just requires a little concentration and thinking to a purpose.

Rehearse Your Talk: Should you rehearse your talk after you have it in some kind of order? By all means. Here is a sure-fire method that is easy and effective. Use the ideas you have selected for your talk in everyday conversation with your friends and business associates. Instead of going over the ball scores, just lean across the luncheon table and say something like this: "You know, Joe, I had an unusual experience one day. I'd like to tell you about it." Joe will probably be happy to listen to your story. Watch him for his reactions. Listen to his response. He may have an interesting idea that may be valuable. He won't know that you are rehearsing your talk, and it really doesn't matter. But he probably will say that he enjoyed the conversation.

Allan Nevins, the distinguished historian, gives similar advice to writers: "Catch a friend who is interested in the subject and talk out what you have learned at length. In this way you discover facts of interpretation that you might have missed, points of arguments that had been unrealized, and the form most suitable for the story you have to tell."

PREDETERMINE YOUR MIND TO SUCCESS

In the first chapter, you remember, this sentence was used in reference to building the right attitude toward public speaking training in general. The same rule applies to the specific task now facing you, that of making each opportunity to speak a successful experience. There are three ways to accomplish this:

Lose Yourself in Your Subject: After you have selected your subject, arranged it according to plan, and rehearsed it by "talking it out" with your friends, your preparation is not ended. You must sell yourself on the importance of your subject You must have the attitude that has inspired all the truly great personages of history—a belief in your cause. How do you fan the fires of faith in your message? By exploring all phases of your subject, grasping its deeper meanings, and asking yourself how your talk will help the audience to be better people for having listened to you.

Keep Your Attention Off Negative Stimuli: For instance, thinking of yourself making errors of grammar or suddenly coming to an end of your talk somewhere in the middle of it is certainly a negative projection that could cancel confidence before you started. It is especially important to keep your attention off yourself just before your turn to speak. Concentrate on what the other speakers are saying, give them your wholehearted attention and you will not be able to work up excessive stage fright.

Give Yourself a Pep Talk: Unless he is consumed by some great cause to which he has dedicated his life, every speaker will experience moments of doubt about his subject matter. He will ask himself whether the topic is the right one for him, whether the audience will be interested in it. He will be sorely tempted to change his subject. At times like these, when negativism is most likely to tear down self-confidence completely, you should give yourself a pep talk. In clear, straightforward terms tell yourself that your talk is the right one for you, because it comes out of your experience, out of your thinking about life. Say to yourself that you are more qualified than any member of the audience to give this particular talk and, by George, you are going to do your best to put it across. Is this old-fashioned Coué teaching? It may be, but modern experimental psychologists now agree that motivation based on autosuggestion is one of the strongest incentives to rapid learning, even when simulated. How much more powerful, then, will be the effect of a sincere pep talk based on the truth?

ACT CONFIDENT

The most famous psychologist that America has produced, Professor William James, wrote as follows:

"Action seems to follow feeling, but really action and feeling go together; and by regulating the action, which is under the more direct control of the will, we can indirectly regulate the feeling, which is not.

"Thus the sovereign voluntary path to cheerfulness, if our spontaneous cheerfulness be lost, is to sit up cheerfully and to act and speak as if cheerfulness were already there. If such conduct does not make you feel cheerful, nothing else on that occasion can.

"So, to feel brave, act as if we were brave, use all of our will to that end, and a courage-fit will very likely replace the fit of fear."

Apply Professor James' advice. To develop courage when you are facing an audience, act as if you already had it. Of course, unless you are prepared, all the acting in the world will avail but little. But granted that you know what you are going to talk about, step out briskly and take a deep breath. In fact, breathe deeply for thirty seconds before you ever face your audience. The increased supply of oxygen will buoy you up and give you courage. The great tenor, Jean de Reszke, used to say that when you had your breath so you "could sit on it", nervousness vanished.

Draw yourself up to your full height and look your audience straight in the eyes, and begin to talk as confidently as if every one of them owed you money. Imagine that they do. Imagine that they have assembled there to beg you for an extension of credit. The psychological effect on you will be beneficial.

If you doubt that this philosophy makes sense, take the

word of an American who will always be a symbol of courage. Once he was the most timorous of men; by practicing self-assurance, he became one of the boldest; he was the trust-busting, audience-swaying, Big-Stick-wielding President of the United States, Theodore Roosevelt.

"Having been a rather sickly and awkward boy," he confesses in his autobiography, "I was, as a young man, at the first both nervous and distrustful of my powers. I had to train myself painfully and laboriously not merely as regards my body but as regards my soul and spirit."

Fortunately, he has disclosed how he achieved the transformation. "When a boy," he wrote, "I read a passage in one of Marryat's books which always impressed me. In this passage, the captain of some small British man-of-war is explaining to the hero how to acquire the quality of fearlessness. He says that at the outset almost every man is frightened when he goes into action, but that the course to follow is for the man to keep such a grip on himself that he can act just as if he were not frightened. After this is kept up long enough, it changes from pretense to reality, and the man does in very fact become fearless by sheer dint of practicing fearlessness when he does not feel it.

"This was the theory upon which I went. There were all kinds of things of which I was afraid at first, ranging from grizzly bears to 'mean' horses and gunfighters; but by acting as if I were not afraid I gradually ceased to be afraid. Most men can have the same experience if they choose."

Overcoming fear of public speaking has a tremendous transfer value to everything that we do. Those who answer this challenge find that they are better persons because of it. They find that their victory over fear of talking before groups has taken them out of themselves into a richer and fuller life.

A salesman wrote: "After a few times on my feet before the class, I felt that I could tackle anyone. One morning I walked up to the door of a particularly tough purchasing agent, and before he could say 'no,' I had my samples spread out on his desk, and he gave me one of the biggest orders I have ever received."

A housewife told one of our representatives: "I was afraid to invite the neighbors in for fear that I wouldn't be able to keep the conversation going. After taking a few sessions and getting up on my feet, I took the plunge and held my first party. It was a great success. I had no trouble stimulating the group along interesting lines of talk."

At a graduating class, a clerk said: "I was afraid of the customers, I gave them a feeling that I was apologetic. After speaking to the class a few times, I found that I was speaking up with more assurance and poise, I began to answer objections with authoritativeness. My sales went up forty-five per cent the first month after I started to speak to this class."

They discovered that it was easy to conquer other fears and anxieties and to be successful where before they may have failed. You, too, will be able to meet the problems and conflicts of life with a new sense of mastery. What has been a series of insoluble situations can become a bright challenge to increased pleasure in living.

Points to Remember

1. Stage fright is a part of public speaking that is felt by all. It is not just you.
2. Rise above rote memorization if you want to be taken seriously.
3. "Fake it till you make it"—Apply the *confidence mantra*.

5

THE VOICE

"Your purpose is to make your audience see what you saw, hear what you heard, feel what you felt. Relevant detail, couched in concrete, colorful language, is the best way to recreate the incident as it happened and to picture it for the audience."

The dramas critic of *The London Times* once declared that acting is nine-tenths voice work. Leaving the message aside, the same may justly be said of public speaking. A rich, correctly-used voice is the greatest physical factor of persuasiveness and power, often over-topping the effects of reason.

But a good voice, well handled, is not only an effective possession for the professional speaker, it is a mark of personal culture as well, and even a distinct commercial asset. Gladstone, himself the possessor of a deep, musical voice, has said: "Ninety men in every hundred in the crowded professions will probably never rise above mediocrity because the training of the voice is entirely neglected and considered of no importance." These are words worth pondering.

FUNDAMENTAL PRINCIPLES FOR GOOD VOICE

There are three fundamental requisites for a good voice:

1. Ease

Signor Bonci of the Metropolitan Opera Company says that the secret of good voice is relaxation; and this is true, for relaxation is the basis of ease. The air waves that produce voice result in a different kind of tone when striking against relaxed muscles than when striking constricted muscles. Try this for yourself. Contract the muscles of your face and throat as you do in hate, and flame out "I hate you!" Now relax as you do when thinking gentle, tender thoughts, and say, "I love you." How different the voice sounds.

In practicing voice exercises, and in speaking, never force your tones. Ease must be your watchword. The voice is a delicate instrument, and you must not handle it with hammer and tongs. Don't make your voice go—let it go. Don't work. Let the yoke of speech be easy and its burden light.

Your throat should be free from strain during speech, therefore it is necessary to avoid muscular contraction. The throat must act as a sort of chimney or funnel for the voice, hence any unnatural constriction will not only harm its tones but injure its health.

Nervousness and mental strain are common sources of mouth and throat constriction, so make the battle for poise and self-confidence for which we pleaded in the opening chapter.

But how can I relax? you ask. By simply willing to relax. Hold your arm out straight from your shoulder. Now—withdraw all power and let it fall. Practice relaxation of the muscles of the throat by letting your neck and head fall forward.

Roll the upper part of your body around, with the waist line acting as a pivot. Let your head fall and roll around as you shift the torso to different positions. Do not force your head around—simply relax your neck and let gravity pull it around as your body moves.

Again, let your head fall forward on your breast; raise your head, letting your jaw hang. Relax until your jaw feels heavy, as though it were a weight hung to your face. Remember, you must relax the jaw to obtain command of it. It must be free and flexible for the moulding of tone, and to let the tone pass out unobstructed.

The lips also must be made flexible, to aid in the moulding of clear and beautiful tones. For flexibility of lips repeat the syllables, mo—me. In saying mo, bring the lips up to resemble the shape of the letter O. In repeating me draw them back as you do in a grin. Repeat this exercise rapidly, giving the lips as much exercise as possible.

Try the following exercise in the same manner:
Mo—E—O—E—OO—Ah.

All the activity of breathing must be centered, not in the throat, but in the middle of the body—you must breathe from the diaphragm. Note the way you breathe when lying flat on the back, undressed in bed. You will observe that all the activity then centers around the diaphragm. This is the natural and correct method of breathing. By constant watchfulness make this your habitual manner, for it will enable you to relax more perfectly the muscles of the throat.

The next fundamental requisite for good voice is openness.

2. Openness

If the muscles of the throat are constricted, the tone passage partially closed, and the mouth kept half-shut, how can you expect the tone to come out bright and clear, or even to come out at all? Sound is a series of waves, and if you make a prison of your mouth, holding the jaws and lips rigidly, it will be very difficult for the tone to squeeze through, and even when it does escape it will lack force and carrying power. Open your mouth wide, relax all the organs of speech, and let the tone flow out easily.

Start to yawn, but instead of yawning, speak while your throat is open. Make this open-feeling habitual when speaking—we say make because it is a matter of resolution and of practice, if your vocal organs are healthy. Your tone passages may be partly closed by enlarged tonsils, adenoids, or enlarged turbinate bones of the nose. If so, a skilled physician should be consulted.

The nose is an important tone passage and should be kept open and free for perfect tones. What we call "talking through the nose" is not talking through the nose, as you can easily demonstrate by holding your nose as you talk. If you are bothered with nasal tones caused by growths or swellings in the nasal passages, a slight, painless operation will remove the obstruction. This is quite important, aside from voice, for the general health will be much lowered if the lungs are continually starved for air.

The final fundamental requisite for good voice is:

3. Forwardness

A voice that is pitched back in the throat is dark, sombre, and unattractive. The tone must be pitched forward, but do not force it forward. You will recall that our first principle was ease. Think the tone forward and out. Believe it is going forward, and allow it to flow easily. You can tell whether you are placing your tone forward or not by inhaling a deep breath and singing ah with the mouth wide open, trying to feel the little delicate sound waves strike the bony arch of the mouth just above the front teeth. The sensation is so slight that you will probably not be able to detect it at once, but persevere in your practice, always thinking the tone forward, and you will be rewarded by feeling your voice strike the roof of your mouth. A correct forward-placing of the tone will do away with the dark, throaty tones that are so unpleasant, inefficient, and harmful to the throat.

Close the lips, humming ng, im, or an. Think the tone forward. Do you feel it strike the lips?

Hold the palm of your hand in front of your face and say vigorously "crash, dash, whirl, buzz". Can you feel the forward tones strike against your hand? Practice until you can. Remember, the only way to get your voice forward is to put it forward.

VOICE SUGGESTIONS

Never attempt to force your voice when hoarse.

Do not drink cold water when speaking. The sudden shock to the heated organs of speech will injure the voice.

Avoid pitching your voice too high—it will make it raspy. This is a common fault. When you find your voice in too high a range, lower it. Do not wait until you get to the platform to try this. Practice it in your daily conversation. Repeat the alphabet, beginning A on the lowest scale possible and going up a note on each succeeding letter, for the development of range. A wide range will give you facility in making numerous changes of pitch.

Do not form the habit of listening to your voice when

speaking. You will need your brain to think of what you are saying—reserve your observation for private practice.

> **Points to Remember**
>
> 1. Follow the fundamental principles for a good voice—ease, openness, forwardness.
> 2. Practice voice exercises on a daily basis.
> 3. To get your voice heard, speak.

6

EFFICIENCY THROUGH CHANGE OF PITCH

"Excitement radiates through your eyes, your face, your voice, your soul, and your whole personality."

By pitch, as everyone knows, we mean the relative position of a vocal tone—as, high, medium, low, or any variation between. In public speech we apply it not only to a single utterance, as an exclamation or a monosyllable (Oh! or the) but to any group of syllables, words, and even sentences that may be spoken in a single tone. This distinction it is important to keep in mind, for the efficient speaker not only changes the pitch of successive syllables, but gives a different pitch to different parts, or word-groups, of successive sentences. It is this phase of the subject which we are considering in this chapter.

EVERY CHANGE IN THE THOUGHT DEMANDS A CHANGE IN THE VOICE-PITCH

Whether the speaker follows the rule consciously, unconsciously, or subconsciously, this is the logical basis upon which all good voice variation is made, yet this law is violated more often than any other by public speakers. A criminal may disregard a law of the state without detection and punishment, but the speaker who violates this regulation suffers its penalty at once in his loss of effectiveness, while his innocent hearers must endure the monotony—for monotony is not only a sin of the perpetrator, as we have shown, but a plague on the victims as well.

Change of pitch is a stumbling block for almost all beginners, and for many experienced speakers also. This is especially true when the words of the speech have been memorized.

If you wish to hear how pitch-monotony sounds, strike the same note on the piano over and over again. You have in your speaking voice a range of pitch from high to low, with a great many shades between the extremes. With all these notes available there is no excuse for offending the ears and taste of your audience by continually using the one note. True, the reiteration of the same tone in music—as in pedal point on an organ composition—may be made the foundation of beauty, for the harmony weaving about that one basic tone produces a consistent, insistent quality not felt in pure variety of chord sequences. In like manner the intoning voice in a ritual may—though it rarely does—possess a solemn beauty. But the public speaker should shun the monotone as he would a pestilence.

CONTINUAL CHANGE OF PITCH IS NATURE'S HIGHEST METHOD

In our search for the principles of efficiency we must continually go back to nature. Listen—really listen—to the birds sing. Which of these feathered tribes are most pleasing in their vocal efforts: those whose voices, though sweet, have little or no range, or those that, like the canary, the lark, and the nightingale, not only possess a considerable range but utter their notes in continual variety of combinations? Even a sweet-toned chirp, when reiterated without change, may grow maddening to the enforced listener.

The little child seldom speaks in a monotonous pitch. Observe the conversations of little folk that you hear on the street or in the home, and note the continual changes of pitch. The unconscious speech of most adults is likewise full of pleasing variations.

Imagine someone speaking the following, and consider if the effect would not be just about as indicated. Remember, we are not now discussing the inflection of single words, but the general pitch in which phrases are spoken.

(High pitch) "I'd like to leave for my vacation tomorrow,— (lower) still, I have so much to do. (Higher) Yet I suppose if I wait until I have time I'll never go."

Repeat this, first in the pitches indicated, and then all in the one pitch, as many speakers would. Observe the difference in naturalness of effect.

CHANGE OF PITCH PRODUCES EMPHASIS

This is a highly important statement. Variety in pitch maintains the hearer's interest, but one of the surest ways to compel attention—to secure unusual emphasis—is to change the pitch of your voice suddenly and in a marked degree. A great contrast always arouses attention. White shows whiter against black; a cannon roars louder in the Sahara silence than in the Chicago hurly burly—these are simple illustrations of the power of contrast.

"What is Congress going to do next?
(High pitch) |
| I do not know."
(Low pitch)

By such sudden change of pitch during a sermon Dr. Newell Dwight Hillis recently achieved great emphasis and suggested the gravity of the question he had raised.

The foregoing order of pitch-change might be reversed with equally good effect, though with a slight change in seriousness—either method produces emphasis when used intelligently, that is, with a common-sense appreciation of the sort of emphasis to be attained.

In attempting these contrasts of pitch it is important to avoid unpleasant extremes. Most speakers pitch their voices too high. One of the secrets of Mr. Bryan's eloquence is his low, bell-like voice. Shakespeare said that a soft, gentle, low voice was "an excellent thing in woman"; it is no less so in man, for a voice need not be blatant to be powerful, and must not be, to be pleasing.

In closing, let us emphasize anew the importance of using variety of pitch. You sing up and down the scale, first touching one note and then another above or below it. Do likewise in speaking.

Thought and individual taste must generally be your guide as to where to use a low, a moderate, or a high pitch. Remember that two sentences, or two parts of the same sentence, which contain changes of thought, cannot possibly be given effectively in the same key. Let us repeat, every big change of thought requires a big change of pitch. What the beginning student will think are big changes of pitch will be monotonously alike. Learn to speak some thoughts in a very high tone—others in a very, very low tone. DEVELOP RANGE. It is almost impossible to use too much of it.

Points to Remember

1. Every change in thought demands a change in your pitch.
2. Shift in pitch is quick to attain the attention of the crowd.
3. Monotone speech is disastrous for a public speaker.

7

HOW TO OPEN A TALK

*"A talk is a voyage. It must be charted.
The speaker who starts nowhere, usually gets there."*

"To foresee is to rule."

That is also a most excellent motto to have on your desk when you are planning your talk. Foresee how you are going to begin when the mind is fresh to grasp every word you utter. Foresee what impression you are going to leave last—when nothing else follows to obliterate it.

Ever since the days of Aristotle, books on this subject have divided the speech into three sections: the introduction, the body, the conclusion. Until comparatively recently, the introduction often was, and could really afford to be, as leisurely as a cart ride. The speaker then was both a bringer of news and an entertainer. A hundred years ago he often filled the niche in the community that is usurped today by the newspaper, the radio, the telephone, the movie theatre.

But conditions have altered amazingly. The world has been made over. Inventions have speeded up life more in the last hundred years than they had formerly in all the ages since Belshazzar and Nebuchadnezzar. Automobiles, aeroplanes, radio; we are moving with increasing speed. And the speaker must fall in line with the impatient tempo of the times. If you are going to use an introduction, believe me, it ought to be short as a billboard advertisement. This is about the temper of the average modern audience: "Got anything to say? All right, let's have it quickly and with very little trimmings. No oratory! Give us the facts quickly and sit down."

When Woodrow Wilson addressed Congress on such a momentous question as an ultimatum on submarine warfare, he announced his topic and centred the audience's attention on the subject with just twenty-three words:

"A situation has arisen in the foreign relations of the country of which it is my plain duty to inform you very frankly."

The salesmanager for the National Cash Register Company opened one of his talks to his men in this fashion. Only three sentences in this introduction; and they are all easy to listen to, they all have vigour and drive:

"You men who get the orders are the chaps who are supposed to keep the smoke coming out of the factory chimney. The volume of smoke emitted from our chimney during the past two summer months hasn't been large enough to darken the landscape to any great extent. Now that the dog days are over and the business-revival season has begun, we are addressing to you a short, sharp request on this subject: We want more smoke."

But do inexperienced speakers usually achieve such commendable swiftness and succinctness in their openings? Strict veracity compels us to record that they do not. The majority of untrained and unskilled speakers will begin in one of two ways—both of which are bad. Let us discuss them forthwith.

THE PITFALLS OF OPENING WITH A SO-CALLED HUMOROUS STORY

For some lamentable reason, the novice often feels that he ought to be funny as a speaker. He may, by nature, mind you, be as solemn as the encyclopædia, utterly devoid of the lighter touch, yet the moment he stands up to talk he imagines he feels, or ought to feel, the spirit of Mark Twain descending upon him. So he is inclined to open with a humorous story, especially if the occasion is an after-dinner affair. What happens? The chances are twenty to one that the narration, the manner of this hardware merchant newly-turned raconteur, is as heavy as the dictionary. The chances are his stories don't "click". In the immortal language of the immortal Hamlet, they prove "weary, stale, flat and unprofitable".

If an entertainer were to misfire a few times like that before a vaudeville audience that had paid for their seats, they would "boo" and shout "give him the bird". But the average group listening to a speaker is very sympathetic; so, out of sheer charity, they will do their best to manufacture a few chuckles while, deep in their hearts, they pity the would-be humorous speaker for his failure! They themselves feel uncomfortable. Haven't you, my dear reader, witnessed this kind of fiasco time after time? The writer has.

In all the difficult realm of speech-making, what is more difficult, more rare, than the ability to make an audience laugh? Humor is a hair-trigger affair; it is so much a matter of individuality, of personality. You are either born with the predilection for being humorous or you are not—much as you are born with or without brown eyes. Not much can be done about either.

Remember, it is seldom the story that is funny of, by, and

in itself. It is the way it is told that makes it a success. Ninety-nine men out of a hundred will fail woefully with the identical stories that made Mark Twain famous. Read the stories that Lincoln repeated in the taverns of the Eighth Judicial District of Illinois, stories that men drove miles to hear, stories that men sat up all night to hear, stories that, according to an eye witness, sometimes caused the natives to "whoop and roll off their chairs". Read those stories aloud to your family and see if you conjure up a smile. Here is one Lincoln used to tell with roaring success. Why not try it? Privately, please—not before an audience. A late traveler, trying to reach home over the muddy roads of the Illinois prairies, was overtaken by a storm. The night was black as ink, the rain descended as if some dam in the heavens had broken, thunder rent the angry clouds like the explosion of dynamite. Chain lightning showed trees falling around. The roar of it was very nearly deafening. Finally a crash more terrific, more terrible than any the helpless man had ever heard in his life, brought him to his knees. He was not given to praying usually, but "Oh, Lord," he gasped, "if it is all the same to you, please give us a little more light and a little less noise."

You may be one of those fortunately endowed individuals who has the rare gift of humor. If so, by all means, cultivate it. You will be thrice welcome wherever you speak. But if your talent lies in other directions, it is folly—and it ought to be high treason—for you to attempt to wear the mantle of Chauncey M. Depew.

Were you to study his speeches, and Lincoln's, and Job Hedges', you would probably be surprised at the few stories they told, especially in their openings. Edwin James Cattell confided to me that he had never told a funny story for the mere sake of humor. It had to be relevant, had to illustrate a point. Humor ought to be merely the frosting on the cake, merely the chocolate between the layers, not the cake itself. Strickland Gillilan, the best humorous lecturer, makes it a rule never to tell a story during the first three minutes of his talk. If he finds that practice advisable, I wonder if you and I would not also.

Must the opening then be heavy-footed, elephantine and excessively solemn? Not at all. Tickle our risibilities, if you can, by some local reference, something anent the occasion or the remarks of some other speaker. Observe some incongruity. Exaggerate it. That brand of humor is forty times more likely to succeed than stale jokes about Pat and Mike, or a mother-in-law, or a goat.

Perhaps the easiest way to create merriment is to tell a joke on yourself. Depict yourself in some ridiculous and embarrassing situation. That gets down to the very essence of much humor. The Eskimos laugh even at a chap who has broken his leg. The Chinese chuckle over the dog that has fallen out of a second storey window and killed himself. We are a bit more sympathetic than that, but don't we smile at the fellow chasing his hat, or slipping on a banana skin?

Almost anyone can make an audience laugh by grouping incongruous ideas or qualities as, for example, the statement of a newspaper writer that he "hated children, tripe, and Democrats".

Note how cleverly Rudyard Kipling raised laughs in this opening to one of his talks in England. He is retailing here, not manufactured anecdotes, but some of his own experiences and playfully stressing their incongruities:

> My Lords, Ladies and Gentlemen: When I was a young man in India I used to report criminal cases for the newspaper that employed me. It was interesting work

because it introduced me to forgers and embezzlers and murderers and enterprising sportsmen of that kind. (Laughter.) Sometimes, after I had reported their trials, I used to visit my friends in jail when they were doing their sentences. (Laughter.) I remember one man who got off with a life sentence for murder. He was a clever, smooth-speaking chap, and he told me what he called the story of his life. He said: "Take it from me that when a man gets crooked, one thing leads to another until he finds himself in such a position that he has to put somebody out of the way to get straight again." (Laughter.) Well, that exactly describes the present position of the cabinet. (Laughter and cheers.)

This is the way William Howard Taft managed a bit of humor at the annual banquet of the superintendents of the Metropolitan Life Insurance Company. The beautiful part of it is this: he is humorous and pays his audience a gracious compliment at the same time:

Mr. *President and Gentlemen of the Metropolitan Life Insurance Company:*

I was out in my old home about nine months ago, and I heard an after-dinner speech there by a gentleman who had some trepidation in making it; and he said he had consulted a friend of his, who had had a great deal of experience in making after-dinner speeches, which friend advised him that the best kind of audience to address, as an after-dinner speaker, was an audience intelligent and well-educated but half-tight. (Laughter and applause.) Now, all I can say is that this audience is one of the best audiences I ever saw for an after-dinner speaker.

Something has made up for the absence of that element that the remark implied (applause), and I must think it is the spirit of the Metropolitan Life Insurance Company. (Prolonged applause.)

DON'T BE APOLOGETIC

The second egregious blunder that the beginner is wont to make in his opening, is this: he apologizes. "I am no speaker… I am not prepared to talk… I have nothing to say…"

Don't! Don't! The opening words of a poem by Kipling are: "There's no use in going further." That is precisely the way an audience feels when a speaker opens in that fashion.

Anyway, if you are not prepared, some of us will discover it without your assistance. Others will not. Why call their attention to it? Why insult your audience by suggesting that you did not think them worth preparing for, that just any old thing you happened to have on the fire would be good enough to serve them? No. No. We don't want to hear your apologies. We are there to be informed and interested, to be *interested*, remember that.

The moment you come before the audience, you have our attention naturally, inevitably. It is not difficult to get it for the first five seconds, but it is difficult to hold it for the next five minutes. If you once lose it, it will be doubly difficult to win it back. So begin with something interesting in your very first sentence. Not the second. Not the third. The first! F-I-R-S-T. First!

"How?" you ask. Rather a large order, I admit. And in attempting to harvest the material to fill it, we must tread our way down devious and dubious paths, for so much depends upon you, upon your audience, your subject, your material, the occasion, and so on. However, we hope that the tentative suggestions discussed and illustrated in the remainder of this chapter will yield something usable and of value.

USE AN EXHIBIT

Perhaps the easiest way in the world to gain attention is to hold up something for people to look at. Even savages and halfwits, and babes in the cradle and monkeys in a zoo and dogs on the street will give heed to that kind of stimulus. It can be used sometimes with effectiveness before the most dignified audience. For example, Mr. S.S. Ellis opened one of his talks by holding a coin between his thumb and forefinger, and high above his shoulder. Naturally everyone looked. Then he inquired: "Has anyone here ever found a coin like this on the pavement? It announces that the fortunate finder will be given a lot free in such and such an estate development. He has but to call and present this coin…" Mr. Ellis then proceeded to reveal the colored man in the cordwood and to condemn the misleading and unethical practices involved.

ASK A QUESTION

Mr. Ellis' opening has another commendable feature. It begins by asking a question, by getting the audience thinking with the speaker, cooperating with him. Note that the *Saturday Evening Post* article on gangsters opens with two questions in the first three sentences: "Are gangsters really organized?… How?" The use of this question-key is really one of the simplest, surest ways to unlock the minds of your audience and let yourself in. When other tools prove useless, you can always fall back on it.

Points to Remember

1. Prepare beforehand the outline of your speech.
2. Stop trying too hard to be funny if you are not.
3. Never apologize to the audience for your presence.

8

SPEAK EFFECTIVELY, THE QUICK AND EASY WAY

> *"It is often dangerous to rush into battle without pausing for preparation or waiting for recruits."*

I seldom watch television in the daytime. But a friend recently asked me to listen to an afternoon show that was directed primarily to housewives. It enjoyed a very high rating, and my friend wanted me to listen because he thought the audience participation part of the show would interest me. It certainly did. I watched it several times, fascinated by the way the master of ceremonies succeeded in getting people in the audience to make talks in a way that caught and held my attention. These people were obviously not professional speakers. They had never been trained in the art of communication. Some of them used poor grammar and mispronounced words. But all of them were interesting. When they started to talk they seemed to lose all fear of being on camera and they held the attention of the audience.

Why was this? I know the answer because I have been employing the techniques used in this program for many years. These people, plain, ordinary men and women, were holding the attention of viewers all over the country; they were talking about themselves, about their most embarrassing moments, their most pleasant memory, or how they met their wives or husbands. They were not thinking of introduction, body, and conclusion. They were not concerned with their diction or their sentence structure. Yet they were getting the final seal of approval from the audience—complete attention in what they had to say. This is dramatic proof of what to me is the first of three cardinal rules for a quick and easy way to learn to speak in public:

SPEAK ABOUT SOMETHING YOU HAVE EARNED THE RIGHT TO TALK ABOUT THROUGH EXPERIENCE OR STUDY

The men and women whose live flesh-and-blood stories made that television program interesting were talking from their own personal experience. They were talking about something they knew. Consider what a dull program would have resulted if they had been asked to define communism or to describe the organizational structure of the United Nations. Yet that is precisely the mistake that countless speakers make at countless meetings and banquets. They decide they must talk about subjects of which they have little or no personal knowledge and to which they have devoted little or no attention. They pick a subject like Patriotism, or Democracy, or Justice, and then, after a few hours of frantic searching through a book of quotations or a speaker's handbook for all occasions, they hurriedly throw together some generalizations vaguely remembered from a political science course they once took in college, and proceed to give a talk distinguished for nothing other than its length. It never occurs to these speakers that the audience might be interested in factual material bringing these high-flown concepts down to earth.

At an area meeting of Dale Carnegie instructors in the Conrad Hilton Hotel in Chicago some years ago, a student speaker started like this: "Liberty, Equality, Fraternity. These are the mightiest ideas in the dictionary of mankind. Without liberty, life is not worth living. Imagine what existence would be like if your freedom of action would be restricted on all sides."

That is as far as he got, because he was wisely stopped by the instructor, who then asked him why he believed what he was saying. He was asked whether he had any proof or personal experience to back up what he had just told us. Then he gave us an amazing story.

He had been a French underground fighter. He told us of the indignities he and his family suffered under Nazi rule. He described in vivid language how he escaped from the secret police and how he finally made his way to America. He ended by saying: "When I walked down Michigan Avenue to this hotel today, I was free to come or go, as I wished. I passed a policeman and he took no notice of me. I walked into this hotel without having to present an identification card, and when this meeting is over I can go anywhere in Chicago I choose to go. Believe me, freedom is worth fighting for." He received a standing ovation from that audience.

TELL US WHAT LIFE HAS TAUGHT YOU

Speakers who talk about what life has taught them never fail to keep the attention of their listeners. I know from experience that speakers are not easily persuaded to accept this point of view—they avoid using personal experiences as too trivial and too restrictive. They would rather soar into the realms of general ideas and philosophical principles, where unfortunately the air is too rarefied for ordinary mortals to breathe. They give us editorials when we are hungry for the news. None of us is averse to listening to editorials, when they are given by a man who has earned the right to editorialize—an editor or publisher of a newspaper. The point, though, is this: Speak on what life has taught you and I will be your devoted listener. It was said of Emerson that he was always willing to listen to any man, no matter how humble his station, because he felt he could learn something from every man he met. I have listened to more adult talks, perhaps, than any other man west of the Iron Curtain, and I can truthfully say that I have never heard a boring talk when the speaker related what life had taught him, no matter how slight or trivial the lesson may have been.

To illustrate: Some years ago, one of our instructors conducted a course in public speaking for the senior officers of New York City banks. Naturally, the members of such a group, having many demands upon their time, frequently found it difficult to prepare adequately, or to do what they conceived of as preparing. All their lives they had been thinking their own individual thoughts, nurturing their own personal convictions, seeing things from their own distinctive angles, living their own original experiences. They had spent forty years storing up material for talks. But it was hard for some of them to realize that.

One Friday a certain gentleman connected with an uptown bank—for our purposes we shall designate him as Mr. Jackson—found four-thirty had arrived, and what was he to talk about? He walked out of his office, bought a copy of *Forbes' Magazine* at a newsstand, and in the subway coming down to the Federal Reserve Bank where the class met, he read an article entitled, "You Have Only Ten Years to Succeed." He read it, not because he was interested in the article especially, but because he had to speak on something to fill his quota of time.

An hour later, he stood up and attempted to talk convincingly and interestingly on the contents of this article.

What was the result, the inevitable result?

He had not digested, had not assimilated what he was trying to say. "Trying to say"—that expresses it precisely. He was *trying*. There was no real message in him seeking for an outlet; and his whole manner and tone revealed it unmistakably. How could he expect the audience to be any more impressed than he himself was? He kept referring to the article, saying the author said so and so. There was a surfeit of *Forbes' Magazine* in it, but regrettably little of Mr. Jackson.

After he finished his talk, the instructor said, "Mr. Jackson, we are not interested in this shadowy personality who wrote that article. He is not here. We can't see him. But we are interested in you and your ideas. Tell us what you think, personally, not what somebody else said. Put more of Mr. Jackson in this. Would you take this same subject next week? Read this article again, and ask yourself whether you agree with the author or not. If you do, illustrate the points of agreement with observations from your own experience. If you don't agree with him, tell us why. Let this article be the starting point from which to launch your own talk."

Mr. Jackson reread the article and concluded that he did not agree with the author at all. He searched his memory for examples to prove his points of disagreement. He developed and expanded his ideas with details from his own experience as a bank executive. He came back the next week and gave a talk that was full of his own convictions, based on his own background. Instead of a warmed-over magazine article, he gave us ore from his own mine, currency coined in his own mint.

I leave it to you to decide which talk made a stronger impact on the class.

BE SURE YOU ARE EXCITED ABOUT YOUR SUBJECT

Not all topics that you and I have earned the right to talk about make us excited. For instance, as a do-it yourself devotee, I certainly am qualified to talk about washing dishes. But somehow or other I can't get excited about this topic. As a matter of fact, I would rather forget about it altogether. Yet I have heard housewives—household executives, that is—give superb talks about this same subject. They have somehow aroused within themselves such a fury of indignation about the eternal task of washing dishes, or they have developed such ingenious methods of getting around this disagreeable chore, that they have become really excited about it. As a consequence, they have been able to talk effectively about this subject of washing dishes. Here is a question that will help you determine the suitability of topics you feel qualified to discuss in public: if someone stood up and directly opposed your point of view, would you be impelled to speak with conviction and earnestness in defense of your position? If you would, you have the right subject for you.

Recently, I came across some notes I had written in 1926 after I had visited the Seventh Session of the League of Nations in Geneva, Switzerland. Here is a paragraph: "After three or four lifeless speakers read their manuscripts, Sir George Foster of Canada took the floor. With immense satisfaction I noted that he had no papers or notes of any kind. He gestured almost constantly. His heart was in what he was saying. He had something he very much wanted to get across. The fact that he was earnestly trying to convey to the audience certain convictions that he cherished in his own heart was as plain as Lake Geneva outside the windows. Principles I have been advocating in my teaching were beautifully illustrated in that talk."

I often recall that speech by Sir George. He was sincere; he was earnest. Only by choosing topics which are felt by the heart as well as thought out by the mind will this sincerity be made manifest. Bishop Fulton J. Sheen, one of America's most dynamic speakers, learned this lesson early in life.

"I was chosen for the debating team in college," he wrote in his book, *Life Is Worth Living*, "and the night before the Notre Dame debate, our professor of debating called me to his office and scolded me.

"'You are absolutely rotten. We have never had anybody in the history of this college who was a worse speaker than yourself.'

"'Well,' I said, trying to justify myself, 'if I am so rotten why did you pick me for the team?'

"'Because,' he answered, 'you can think; not because you can talk. Get over in that corner. Take a paragraph of your speech and go through it.' I repeated a paragraph over and over again for an hour, at the end of which he said, 'Do you see any mistake in that?' 'No.' Again an hour and a half, two hours, two and a half hours, at the end of which I was exhausted. He said, 'Do you still not see what is wrong?'

"Being naturally quick, after two hours and a half, I caught on. I said, 'Yes, I am not sincere. I am not myself. I do not talk as if I meant it.'"

At this point, Bishop Sheen learned a lesson he always remembered: *he put himself into his talk*. He became excited about his subject matter. Only then the wise professor said, "Now, you are ready to speak!"

When a member of one of our classes says, "I don't get excited about anything, I lead a humdrum sort of life," our instructors are trained to ask him what he does in his spare time. One goes to the movies, another bowls, and another cultivates roses. One man told his instructor that he collected books of matches. As the instructor continued to question him about this unusual hobby, he gradually became animated. Soon he was using gestures as he described the cabinets in which he stored his collection. He told his instructor that he had match books from almost every country in the world. When he became excited about his favorite topic, the instructor stopped him. "Why don't you tell us about this subject? It sounds fascinating to me." He said that he didn't think anyone would be interested! Here was a man who had spent years in pursuit of a hobby that was almost a passion with him; yet he was negative about its value as a topic to speak about. This instructor assured this man that the only way to gauge the interest value of a subject was to ask yourself how interested you are in it. He talked that night with all the fervor of the true collector, and I heard later that he gained a certain amount of local recognition by going to various luncheon clubs and talking about match book collecting.

This illustration leads directly to the third guiding principle for those who want a quick and easy way to learn to speak in public.

BE EAGER TO SHARE YOUR TALK WITH YOUR LISTENERS

There are three factors in every speaking situation: the speaker, the speech or the message, and the audience. The first two rules in this chapter dealt with the interrelationships of the speaker to a speech. Up to this point there is no speaking situation.

Only when the speaker relates his talk to a living audience will the speaking situation come to life. The talk may be well prepared; it may concern a topic which the speaker is excited about; but for complete success, another factor must enter into his delivery of the talk. He must make his listeners feel that what he has to say is important to them. He must not only be excited about his topic, but he must be eager to transfer this excitement to his listeners. In every public speaker of note in the history of eloquence, there has been this unmistakable quality of salesmanship, evangelism, call it what you will. The effective speaker earnestly desires his listeners to feel what he feels, to agree with his point of view, to do what he thinks is right for them to do, and to enjoy and relive his experience with him. He is audience-centered and not self-centered. He knows that the success or failure of his talk is not for him to decide—it will be decided in the minds and hearts of his hearers.

I trained a number of men in the New York City Chapter of the American Institute of Banking to speak during a thrift campaign. One of the men in particular wasn't getting across to his audience. The first step in helping that man was to fire up his mind and heart with zeal for his subject. I told him to go off by himself and to think over this subject until he became enthusiastic about it. I asked him to remember that the Probate Court Records in New York show that more than 85 per cent of the people leave nothing at all at death; that only 3.3 per cent leave $10,000 or over. He was to keep constantly in mind that he was not asking people to do him a favor or something that they could not afford to do. He was to say to himself: "I am preparing these people to have meat and bread and clothes and comfort in their old age, and to leave their wives and children secure." He had to remember he was going out to perform a great social service. In short, he had to be a crusader.

He thought over these facts. He burned them into his mind. He aroused his own interest, stirred his own enthusiasm, and came to feel that he, indeed, had a mission. Then, when he went out to talk, there was a ring to his words that carried conviction. He sold his listeners on the benefits of thrift because he had an eager desire to help people. He was no longer just a speaker armed with facts; he was a missionary seeking converts to a worthwhile cause.

At one time in my teaching career I relied considerably on the textbook rules of public speaking. In doing this I was merely reflecting some of the bad habits that had been instilled into me by teachers who had not broken away from the stilted mechanics of elocution.

I shall never forget my first lesson in speaking. I was taught to let my arm hang loosely at my side, with the palm turned to the rear, fingers half-closed and thumb touching my leg. I was drilled to bring the arm up in a picturesque curve, to give the wrist a classical turn, and then to unfold the forefinger first, the second finger next, and the little finger last. When the whole aesthetic and ornamental movement had been executed, the arm was to retrace the course of the curve and rest again by the side of the leg. The whole performance was wooden and affected. There was nothing sensible or honest about it.

My instructor made no attempt to get me to put my own individuality into my speaking; no attempt to have me speak like a normal, living human being conversing in an energetic manner with my audience.

Contrast this mechanistic approach to speech training with the three primary rules I have been discussing in this chapter. They are the basis of my entire approach to training in effective speaking. You will come across them again and again in this book.

Points to Remember

1. Make your speech authentic and relatable by speaking about your personal experiences.
2. Three factors of public speaking: speaker, speech and audience.
3. Enthusiasm is contagious. Be excited about your subject and the crowd will be too.

9

EXPRESSING GENUINE INTEREST IN OTHERS

*"You can make more friends in two months by becoming
interested in other people than you can in two years
by trying to get other people interested in you."*

Lynn Povich, editor-in-chief of *Working Woman* magazine, spent twenty-five years of her life at *Newsweek*. She started as a secretary, moved up to researcher, and eventually became the first woman ever named a *Newsweek* senior editor. This put her in the position of supervising writers and editors she had once worked for as a researcher. "It was an interesting turn of events," Povich says.

Most of her colleagues reacted quite well to the promotion, all except one of the six section editors who now reported to her. Povich recalls, "He was against the idea from the very beginning—not because he disliked me, but because he felt that I had gotten the job only because I am a woman and that I probably didn't have the credentials for it. He didn't say anything to me, but I heard from several other people that that's what he thought."

Povich tried not to let this bother her. She immersed herself in the new job. She helped develop story ideas. She spent time talking to the writers. She expressed a sincere interest in each of the sections she was responsible for—medicine, media, television, religion, lifestyle, and ideas.

Then one day, about six months after Povich's appointment, her big critic walked into her office and sat in a chair across from her desk. "I have to tell you something," he said to her. "I was totally against this move. I thought you were too young. I thought you didn't have the experience. I thought you got the promotion only because you were a woman.

"But I want to say I really appreciate the interest you've shown in the work, in the writers, and in the section editors. I've had four guys who were senior editors before you. It was clear to me they were all using this as a stepping-stone for the next position. None of them genuinely cared. It's absolutely clear that you really are interested, and you show that interest to everyone."

Not surprisingly, Povich has brought that same management style—developed over the years—into her new job at *Working Woman*. "You have to take people seriously," she explains. "First of all, you can't be remote. You have to touch base with them on a regular basis. I do a lot of walking around and talking to people. We have a system of regular meetings so that everyone here knows there's a particular time, a particular week, when they're actually going to be alone with me. They'll have their time to say whatever they want to. I'm available. I'm interested in what they're doing, I'm interested in their work, and I'm interested in them as people."

Expressing genuine interest in others—there's no better way to make people interested in you. People respond to people who are sincerely interested in them. They can't help but respond.

This is one of the most basic facts of human psychology. We are flattered by other people's attention. It makes us feel special.

It makes us feel important. We want to be around people who show interest in us. We want to keep them close. We tend to reciprocate their interest by showing interest in them.

Monsignor Tom Hartman has become something of a legend among young Roman Catholics on Long Island, New York. He has, over the years, been asked to perform more than thirty-eight hundred weddings and to baptize more than ten thousand newborn babies. Why do all these people keep turning to the Monsignor? Aren't there any other priests out there to choose from? Of course there are, but few manage to show the intense interest in other people that Hartman is so well know for.

Hartman doesn't preside over assembly-line wedding ceremonies. He takes a more studied, individual, personal approach. He wants to know everything he possibly can about the two people who have come to him to be married. He invites them to the rectory.

He visits their homes. Over a period of several months, he leads them through a series of conversations about themselves. That way, he can tailor a wedding that will fit their personal interests and needs.

"Yes, I'll do your wedding," he tells these couples, "but I don't want it to be just a ritual. I want to discover the mystery here. I want this to be the best wedding possible for you. I want to know about you. I want to talk with you about what you've discovered about your relationship, what you love about each other. I want to learn about the struggles you've had and how you got through those struggles. And I'm going to communicate that at your wedding."

A Hartman wedding isn't the quickest and easiest trip to the altar. But Hartman's personal interest pays major dividends for these couples. Through his caring, they learn new things about each other. "When people see that I am so interested in an important moment in their lives, they began to listen to me on other levels too," he said.

Hartman takes the same personal approach when asked to perform a baptism. He wants to know about the family, about the child, about all the things that make this birth so special to those involved. He has gone so far as to attend Lamaze classes with one single mother whose baby he was going to baptize.

That one expression of interest, he says, has given him an added degree of credibility when he encourages prospective fathers to go through this preparation as well. By attending classes himself, Hartman says, "I was able to get on the trust level with so many men and say, 'Do it. It will introduce you to mystery.' Many men have come back to me later, thrilled they'd done it, and said, 'If I never had that experience, I would be on the outside looking in.'"

There are many different ways of showing interest, and most of them are much easier than attending Lamaze classes. An expression of interest can be as simple as using a pleasant voice on the telephone. When someone calls, say hello in a tone that implies, "I'm happy to hear from you." When you see a familiar face at the shopping mall, greet the person and express a genuine pleasure at the coincidence.

Smile at people. Learn their names and how to pronounce them. Get the spellings and the titles right. Remember their birthdays. Ask about their husbands and wives and children. "I always knew that Clarence Michalis was at Bristol-Myers," says David S. Taylor, secretary-treasurer of H.G. Wellington & Company, Inc., an investment-brokerage firm. "The minute we met, that would click. I remember those two things together. Not everybody does. I have a memory bank that would connect people with businesses."

You never know when these names will come in handy.

Taylor learned this lesson when he was working as an executive in the beverage industry. "When I worked for Canada Dry," he said, "it may be hard to think why, but it was important for me to know people in the airline industry. They were a big customer. Grumman Aircraft fed a lot of people, and they had a lot of vending machines that dispensed drinks.

"It was just an entree. You could call up and say, 'Look, I'm having a problem with such-and-such.' Remembering these names and having those connections was enormously helpful."

Taylor used this technique as the basis for forming genuine relationships with people. By taking the time to remember people's names and associations, he has been able to help bring people together and solve their problems.

Don't limit those expressions of interest to the so-called important people in your life. Chances are they already get plenty of attention. Don't forget the secretaries, the assistants, the receptionists, the messengers, and all the other underrecognized people who keep your life on track. Ask about their days. It's the right thing to do—and you'll be surprised how much quicker the mail arrives at your desk in the morning.

Interest in people has always been a personal trademark of Adriana Bitter, president of Scalamandré Silks. One day Bitter was walking through the wallpaper-print area. She overheard the head of Scalamandré's wallpaper department talking to an employee.

"How are you, Louie?" the department head asked.

"Oh, not too well," Louie answered. "I've been suffering from a depression."

"Do you know why?" Bitter asked him, walking up.

"I have this fear of heights and fear of being closed in," Louie explained. "I have to get on a plane and fly to Puerto Rico for my Christmas vacation, and I'm frightened."

Bitter asked a few more questions. "I think it's a good idea if you see a doctor about this," she said finally.

"I went to see a doctor, and I had to go up to the thirty-second floor, and I was so afraid."

"Maybe you'd better find a doctor on the first floor," Bitter told him.

"You know, I had a dream the other night, Mrs. Bitter," he said. "I dreamed that I was so frightened, and you came up and put your arms around me and told me not to worry."

So Bitter put her arms around him and said, "Don't worry, Louie. It will go away. Take some deep breaths."

They talked some more. He started to laugh, and he said, "Will you come on the plane with me?"

Bitter laughed with him.

"He left yesterday," she said a few days later. "So I guess he's doing fine."

People will respond immediately to a genuine expression of warmth. So be sincere. Honest, heartfelt interest has to be built up over time.

A great way to open a conversation—even a business conversation—is to notice an item that relates somehow to the person you're speaking with. It could be a drawing on the office wall, a desktop pencil holder made by a child, a squash racquet leaning in the corner of the room. Make a comment that shows interest, admiration, or warmth. Or ask a question of a similar kind. "That's a beautiful picture. Who's the artist?" Or "What a thoughtful gift. Is that from one of your children?" Or "Squash? Isn't that a hard game to learn?" There's nothing profound about any of those remarks. But every one of them shows a basic, personal interest in the other person, and it connects in a positive, tasteful way.

Such displays of interest are the fundamental building

blocks of successful human relationships. They are the little details that say, "You are important to me. I'm interested. I care." Very few people in this world mind hearing that.

Everything was going well for Steven and Robin Weiser. Steven ran a successful insurance agency. They had a lovely suburban home. He was a consistently generous philanthropist. The couple's oldest daughter was in her first year at Yale, and the younger twins were doing great in high school.

Then one Saturday night as Steven and Robin were eating at a restaurant, he had a massive heart attack and died. He was just forty-five years old.

The funeral was packed with hundreds of people Steve Weiser had touched—his friends, his business associates, officials from the many charities he supported. Many of these people made condolence calls at the Weiser home.

What was nearly as shocking as Steven's untimely death was something his wife said that night. "It's a shame that Steven didn't know how many people he touched, how many people loved him," Robin Weiser said.

Steven Weiser? With all those friends and associates? After all that charity work? Apparently few of these people had ever told him how they felt.

Don't make the same mistake. When you care about someone—a friend, a spouse, a colleague—by all means let that person know. And do it while you have the chance.

Even more important than expressing interest is showing it. Harrison Conference Services, Inc., is in the business of organizing meetings and seminars, worrying about all the logistics so the clients can keep their minds focused on the real work at hand. To thrive, a company like Harrison must show its guests, over and over again, that the staff is genuinely—almost singlemindedly—interested in them.

It's not enough to have beautiful conference facilities, as Harrison certainly does. It's not enough to have attractive rooms, first-rate cuisine, high-tech audiovisual equipment, or a plethora of recreational choices, all of which Harrison has. Unless the guests feel they're being treated with genuine interest and respect, they'll take their business elsewhere.

"I remember a guest who was attending one of our international programs, a man from China," says Walter A. Green, Harrison's chairman. "One of our people, a hostess, overheard him saying he missed the food of his native country. Well, the hostess happened to be a Chinese chef on the side. The next day she went home and prepared some special Chinese food," and brought the dishes into work. "I can't tell you how taken he seemed by this personal concern for his comfort and by the thrill of being able to share his own cuisine with the people at his table."

What the hostess's action said was, "We are interested—genuinely interested, consistently interested—in you." Who wouldn't appreciate that kind of attention?

Thankfully, this way of relating is a habit easily learned and very gratifying. All it takes is the realization of how important it is and a little bit of practice. Try it with the next person you meet: "Whatever happened to that summer house you were thinking of buying?" Or "What a great view you have in here. How do you stop yourself from staring out the window all day?"

Once you start this process, it will quickly become a natural part of your life. Before you know it, you'll be expressing interest, showing interest, and really becoming more interested in the people around you. The added benefit is that a genuine interest in others will take you outside yourself and make you less focused on whatever your own problems are.

The more you stay focused on other people, the more

rewarding your personal relationships will be and the fewer negative thoughts you will have. Not a bad payback for a few kind words.

Best-selling business author Harvey B. Mackay started out his career in the envelope industry. That's where he learned many of the lessons that make up his best-selling books. "I'm very strong on creative gifts," Mackay says, "and when I say a gift, I'm not talking about something that's expensive and costs money."

Mackay had an envelope salesman, "a man who in my judgment was just a C-plus salesman," he recalls. "I remember him telling me that one of his buyers had a baby girl, so he went down and bought a gift. Fine, that's wonderful. But the gift was not for the baby girl. It was for the jealous brother at home. He was a year and half, just a piddly little thing. But I remember, that one creative gesture stuck with me right away. All of a sudden I didn't think of him as a C-plus anymore. Now he's our key sales manager."

Expressing this kind of interest in others is especially important when you're the new kid on the block. It was as if Bill Clinton already knew that when he showed up for his first day of kindergarten. He was, his teacher has said, naturally friendly and disarmingly interested in the other children.

"Hi," he went around saying. "I'm Bill. What's your name?" Corny? Maybe. But then none of his classmates in Hope, Arkansas, expressed any surprise when little Billy was elected president of the United States.

An open, friendly, interested greeting is just as important when you're the new person in the office or the new business-owner in town. The message should not be, I'm here, now what can you do for me? It should be instead, I'm here, now what can I do for you?

So volunteer at the local hospital. Sign up as a Little League coach. Join the PTA. Get involved in a local charity. These are all ways of showing interest in the community, of saying, "I care about this place." Any one of these will help you meet new people in a comfortable environment. It will be fun. It will make you feel good about yourself. It will help you develop new relationships, gain self-confidence, and it will bring you out of your comfort zone.

Stephen Ghysels, who is now a vice president at the Bank of America, learned the hard way how important it is to take a genuine interest in others.

Ghysels got an impressively early start on the fast track. Back in the late 1980s, fresh out of college, he was already an officer at a large investment firm. He had an Art Deco condo on the west side of Los Angeles and a Mercedes in the driveway—all by age 25. "I thought I had it all and I let people know. I had a real attitude.

"But just as the recession was approaching in 1990," Ghysels says, "my boss called me into the office and said, 'Steve, it's not your performance. It's your attitude. People in this office just don't like working with you. I'm afraid we are going to have to part company.'

"It hit me like a rock. I, Mr. Success, was being fired. I knew it wouldn't take me very long to find another high-paying executive position. Wrong. Welcome to the recession, Steve!

"After several frustrating months of job searching, the attitude layer peeled off and revealed a thick layer of fear. For the first time in my life I lacked confidence and was gripped by an intense fear. Since I had previously alienated everyone, I had nowhere to turn, no one to talk to. I was alone."

Only then did Ghysels learn to be interested in others. He started listening. He started caring about something other than himself. He gained a perspective on his own trouble, meeting people who were far worse off than himself. He opened himself up and became more human, more likable, and infinitely more employable.

"I began to look at other people in a different light," he recalls. "My attitude changed. I felt differently. My fear was reduced. My mind was opened. And people began to take notice. The quality of my life was better, even though I had to sell the condo and the Mercedes.

"Three years later, I once again have an officer-level job—only this time I'm surrounded by coworkers I can honestly call my friends."

> THERE'S NOTHING MORE EFFECTIVE AND REWARDING THAN SHOWING A GENUINE INTEREST IN OTHER PEOPLE.

Points to Remember

1. The quickest way to make people interested in you is by showing your interest in them.
2. Make the effort to learn the name of the person you are interacting with, such small gestures go a long way.
3. Be a good listener, to be an even better speaker.

10

CONCENTRATION IN DELIVERY

> *"Concentration is a process of distraction from less important matters."*

A fault in public speakers that is as pernicious as it is common is that they try to think of the succeeding sentence while still uttering the former, and in this way their concentration trails off; in consequence, they start their sentences strongly and end them weakly. In a well-prepared written speech the emphatic word usually comes at one end of the sentence. But an emphatic word needs emphatic expression, and this is precisely what it does not get when concentration flags by leaping too soon to that which is next to be uttered. Concentrate all your mental energies on the present sentence. Remember that the mind of your audience follows yours very closely, and if you withdraw your attention from what you are saying to what you are going to say, your audience will also withdraw theirs. They may not do so consciously and deliberately, but they will surely cease to give importance to the things that you yourself slight. It is fatal to either the actor or the speaker to cross his bridges too soon.

Of course, all this is not to say that in the natural pauses of your speech you are not to take swift forward surveys—

they are as important as the forward look in driving a motor car; the caution is of quite another sort: while speaking one sentence do not think of the sentence to follow. Let it come from its proper source—within yourself. You cannot deliver a broadside without concentrated force—that is what produces the explosion. In preparation you store and concentrate thought and feeling; in the pauses during delivery you swiftly look ahead and gather yourself for effective attack; during the moments of actual speech, SPEAK—DON'T ANTICIPATE. Divide your attention and you divide your power.

This matter of the effect of the inner man upon the outer needs a further word here, particularly as touching concentration.

"What do you read, my lord?" Hamlet replied, "Words. Words. Words." That is a world-old trouble. The mechanical calling of words is not expression, by a long stretch. Did you ever notice how hollow a memorized speech usually sounds? You have listened to the ranting, mechanical cadence of inefficient actors, lawyers and preachers. Their trouble is a mental one—they are not concentratedly thinking thoughts that cause words to issue with sincerity and conviction, but are merely enunciating word-sounds mechanically. Painful experience alike to audience and to speaker! A parrot is equally eloquent. Again let Shakespeare instruct us, this tune in the insincere prayer of the King, Hamlet's uncle. He laments thus pointedly:

> My words fly up, my thoughts remain below:
> Words without thoughts never to heaven go.

The truth is, that as a speaker your words must be born again every time they are spoken, then they will not suffer in their utterance, even though perforce committed to memory and repeated, like Dr. Russell Conwell's lecture, Acres of Diamonds, five thousand times. Such speeches lose nothing by repetition for the perfectly patent reason that they arise from concentrated thought and feeling and not a mere necessity for saying something—which usually means anything, and that, in turn, is tantamount to nothing. If the thought beneath your words is warm, fresh, spontaneous, a part of yourself, your utterance will have breath and life. Words are only a result. Do not try to get the result without stimulating the cause.

Do you ask how to concentrate? Think of the word itself, and of its philological brother, concentric. Think of how a lens gathers and concenters the rays of light within a given circle. It centers them by a process of withdrawal. It may seem like a harsh saying, but the man who cannot concentrate is either weak of will, a nervous wreck, or has never learned what will-power is good for.

You must concentrate by resolutely withdrawing your attention from everything else. If you concentrate your thought on a pain which may be afflicting you, that pain will grow more intense. Count your blessings and they will multiply. Center your thought on your strokes and your tennis play will gradually improve. To concentrate is simply to attend to one thing, and attend to nothing else. If you find that you cannot do that, there is something wrong—attend to that first. Remove the cause and the symptom will disappear. Cultivate your will by willing and then doing, at all costs. Concentrate—and you will win.

Points to Remember

1. Focus on not the words you are uttering, but the thought process behind those words.
2. Don't start forming your next sentence when you have not completed the current one. Stay with the audience—in the present.
3. Will yourself to concentrate on the task at hand and you will achieve it.

11

METHODS OF DELIVERY

"To develop courage when you are facing an audience, act as if you already have it."

There are four fundamental methods of delivering an address; all others are modifications of one or more of these: reading from manuscript, committing the written speech and speaking from memory, speaking from notes, and extemporaneous speech. It is impossible to say which form of delivery is best for all speakers in all circumstances—in deciding for yourself you should consider the occasion, the nature of the audience, the character of your subject, and your own limitations of time and ability. However, it is worthwhile warning you not to be lenient in self-exaction. Say to yourself courageously: "What others can do, I can attempt". A bold spirit conquers where others flinch, and a trying task challenges pluck.

READING FROM MANUSCRIPT

This method really deserves short shrift in a book on public speaking, for, delude yourself as you may, public reading is not public speaking. Yet there are so many who grasp this broken reed for support that we must here discuss the "read speech"—

apologetic misnomer as it is.

Certainly there are occasions—among them, the opening of Congress, the presentation of a sore question before a deliberative body, or a historical commemoration—when it may seem not alone to the "orator" but to all those interested that the chief thing is to express certain thoughts in precise language—in language that must not be either misunderstood or misquoted. At such times oratory is unhappily elbowed to a back bench, the manuscript is solemnly withdrawn from the capacious inner pocket of the new frock coat, and everyone settles himself resignedly, with only a feeble flicker of hope that the so-called speech may not be as long as it is thick. The words may be golden, but the hearer's eyes are prone to be leaden, and in about one instance out of a hundred does the perpetrator really deliver an impressive address. His excuse is his apology—he is not to be blamed, as a rule, for someone decreed that it would be dangerous to cut loose from manuscript moorings and take his audience with him on a really delightful sail.

One great trouble on such "great occasions" is that the essayist—for such he is—has been chosen not because of his speaking ability but because his grandfather fought in a certain battle, or his constituents sent him to Congress, or his gifts in some line of endeavor other than speaking have distinguished him.

As well choose a surgeon from his ability to play golf. To be sure, it always interests an audience to see a great man; because of his eminence they are likely to listen to his words with respect, perhaps with interest, even when droned from a manuscript. But how much more effective such a deliverance would be if the papers were cast aside!

Nowhere is the read-address so common as in the pulpit—the pulpit, that in these days least of all can afford to invite a handicap. Doubtless many clergymen prefer finish to fervor—let them choose: they are rarely men who sway the masses to acceptance of their message. What they gain in precision and elegance of language they lose in force.

There are just four motives that can move a man to read his address or sermon:

1. Laziness is the commonest. Enough said. Even heaven cannot make a lazy man efficient.
2. A memory so defective that he really cannot speak without reading. Alas, he is not speaking when he is reading, so his dilemma is painful—and not to himself alone. But no man has a right to assume that his memory is utterly bad until he has buckled down to memory culture—and failed. A weak memory is oftener an excuse than a reason.
3. A genuine lack of time to do more than write the speech. There are such instances—but they do not occur every week! The disposition of your time allows more flexibility than you realize. Motive 3 too often harnesses up with Motive 1.
4. A conviction that the speech is too important to risk forsaking the manuscript. But, if it is vital that every word should be so precise, the style so polished, and the thoughts so logical that the preacher must write the sermon entire, is not the message important enough to warrant extra effort in perfecting its delivery? It is an insult to a congregation and disrespectful to Almighty God to put the phrasing of a message above the message itself. To reach the hearts of the hearers the sermon must be delivered—it is only half delivered when the speaker cannot utter it with

original fire and force, when he merely repeats words that were conceived hours or weeks before and hence are like champagne that has lost its fizz. The reading preacher's eyes are tied down to his manuscript; he cannot give the audience the benefit of his expression. How long would a play fill a theater if the actors held their cue-books in hand and read their parts? Imagine Patrick Henry reading his famous speech; Peter-the-Hermit, manuscript in hand, exhorting the crusaders; Napoleon, constantly looking at his papers, addressing the army at the Pyramids; or Jesus reading the Sermon on the Mount! These speakers were so full of their subjects, their general preparation had been so richly adequate, that there was no necessity for a manuscript, either to refer to or to serve as "an outward and visible sign" of their preparedness. No event was ever so dignified that it required an artificial attempt at speech making. Call an essay by its right name, but never call it a speech. Perhaps the most dignified of events is a supplication to the Creator. If you ever listened to the reading of an original prayer you must have felt its superficiality.

Regardless of what the theories may be about manuscript delivery, the fact remains that it does not work out with efficiency. Avoid it whenever possible.

Points to Remember

1. The four fundamental methods of delivery: reading a manuscript, reciting from memory, speaking from notes, extemporaneous speech.
2. Public reading is not public speaking.
3. What you lack in experience, make up for in practice and confidence.

12

THE POWER OF ENTHUSIASM

"Is enthusiasm important in selling? Yes, genuine, heartfelt enthusiasm is one of the most potent factors of success in almost any undertaking."

If enthusiasm can cause a group of intelligent business people to ignore the basic laws of science, just imagine what it can do if someone is actually making sense.

Here is the bottom line on enthusiasm: it's infectious, and it makes people respond. This is true in the classroom, in the boardroom, and on the campaign trail. It's just as true in the ice-hockey rink. If you are not enthusiastic about an idea or a project, nobody else will ever be. If the leaders don't believe enthusiastically in the direction of a company, don't ever expect the employees or the customers or Wall Street to. The best way to get someone excited about an idea—or a project or a campaign—is to be excited yourself. And to show it.

Tommy Draffen had just taken a new job as a salesman with Culver Electronics Sales, a California importer of intercom speakers. According to the longstanding company practice, this meant one thing: Draffen was handed a list of incredibly tough prospects. There was one firm in particular that used to be a big Culver customer but had been lost years ago.

"I decided to make getting their business a personal challenge," Draffen says. "That meant convincing my company president that we could get the business back. He was not as sure as I was, but he didn't want to throttle back my enthusiasm. So he allowed me to visit the customer."

Draffen turned this account into a personal mission. He offered guaranteed pricing, reduced lead time, and better service. He assured the company's director of purchasing that Culver would do "whatever it takes to satisfy your needs."

The key to Draffen's enthusiasm came during his first face-to-face meeting with the purchasing director. He walked into the meeting with a smile on his face, and he said, "Glad to be back. We're going to make this work together."

Draffen never once thought he would not close this deal. He all but ignored the fact that his company had already lost this account. With an upbeat, enthusiastic attitude, he convinced the client that Culver was ready to serve again.

"As it turns out, the purchasing manager later told our president the only reason they were entertaining our offers was because of my enthusiasm. They gave us the order that will turn out to be half a million dollars a year."

Before another word is written on the subject of enthusiasm, let's clarify a widespread misconception once and for all. Loudness does not equal enthusiasm. Nor does pounding on the table, or jumping up and down, or acting like a fool. That's fake. It's obvious. It doesn't fool anyone. It almost always does more harm than good.

Enthusiasm is a feeling that has to come from inside. This concept is so important, it's worth saying again. *Enthusiasm is a feeling that has to come from inside.* It's not to be confused with boisterous hype.

It's true, increased physical movement and stronger voice

projection sometimes accompany an inner feeling of enthusiasm. But people who indulge in superanimation—you know, "I'm great, you're great, we're all so great today!"—might as well wear a big I'm a Phony badge instead.

"Leadership starts out with the whole issue of integrity and credibility," says Ray Stata, the Analog Devices chairman. "So you have to be believed and believable. You have to be a person who honors his or her word, a person whom people can trust. I think those are prerequisites for open dialogue, as opposed to seeming manipulative or gladhanding or insensitive or whatever."

The real enthusiasts of history understood this intuitively. Back in the 1950s, was Jonas Salk enthusiastic about creating a polio vaccine? Of course he was. He dedicated years of his life to the pursuit. Anyone who came in contact with Salk could see his enthusiasm immediately in the way his eyes lit up when he spoke about his research, in the round-the-clock sessions he led in the lab. Salk became an inspiration for two generations of scientists. Yes, the man positively exuded enthusiasm, but Salk did not rant and rave. Now he's devoting that very same enthusiasm to finding a vaccine for the HIV virus, the one that causes AIDS.

In 1969 Neil Armstrong was just as enthusiastic about walking on the moon. The enthusiasm was palpable even in his flat Ohio voice. "That's one small step for man," he said, "one giant leap for mankind." Armstrong didn't need to shout the sentence or do a little jig before climbing back to the Apollo spacecraft. But enthusiasm was obviously jampacked in Armstrong's thoughtful words.

In 1991, when General Norman Schwarzkopf led American troops in the Persian Gulf War, did he seem nonchalant? Not by a long shot. He didn't have to scream and shout at his troops to make them see he believed in their mission. You could just tell in a five-second news clip on CNN.

None of these great enthusiasts was especially loud or boisterous. But they left no one wondering how they felt about their work.

True enthusiasm is made of two parts: eagerness and assurance. Be excited about something and express confidence in your ability to handle it. That's all enthusiasm takes. Have those two feelings about a company, a project, or an idea, and your enthusiasm will be dangerously contagious. You'll have it. Others will know you have it. Pretty soon, they'll have *it*, too. Guaranteed.

"Enthusiasm is something that always came naturally to me," says Olympic gymnast Mary Lou Retton. "I'm just a very positive person, and I've always surrounded myself with positive people. That's important for me."

That positive outlook was part of Retton's secret for getting through all the grueling training sessions she had to endure as a young world-class gymnast. "There were times when my coach, Bela Karolyi, was in a bad mood and was very strict in the gym. I would try to keep our group of four or five girls positive. But if you had one girl who was down and said, 'Gosh, I don't want to do this,' it would bring everybody down. I hated that. You could have ten people who were in the best possible mood, but if you have that one negative person, you'd bring the whole group down. So I'd try and steer away from those people."

"Always surround yourself with happy, successful people," agrees Harvey Mackay, the business-book author. "I don't go around with negative people. If your friends and your peers and the people you respect and the people that you're reading about are upbeat, enthusiastic, confident people with a lot of self-esteem, that will also become a part of you."

ENTHUSIASM—NOT SOMETHING YOU ARE BORN WITH

It is almost impossible to underestimate the power of enthusiasm. "Every great and commanding movement is the triumph of enthusiasm," Ralph Waldo Emerson once said. "Nothing great was ever achieved without it." This was true of the civil rights movement. It was true of the founding of America. It is just as true of all big companies today.

Enthusiasm is as important as high ability, as important as hard work. We all know people who are brilliant and accomplish nothing. We all know people who work hard and get nowhere. But people who work hard, love their jobs, and convey enthusiasm—those are the ones who are going places.

"The difference in actual skill and ability and intelligence between those who succeed and those who fail is usually neither wide nor striking," said Frederick D. Williamson, president of the New York Central Railway. "But if two people are nearly equally matched, the one who is enthusiastic will find the scales tipped in his favor. And a person who has second-rate ability with enthusiasm will often outstrip someone of first-rate ability without enthusiasm."

The chief failing of IQ tests has always been that they don't measure a person's enthusiasm or emotional drive. When these tests were first introduced two generations ago, they were touted as amazing predictive tools. By measuring someone's "intelligence quotient," you could predict with great precision what that person would be able to achieve in life, or so the IQ testing companies claimed.

If only life were as simple as that. The idea was alluring, especially at a time when the whole world was placing more of its faith in science. The standardized-testing business took off. College admissions officers relied on the tests slavishly to determine who was worth accepting. School guidance counselors used them to steer youngsters into advanced or remedial work. The military used the IQ tests to decide who was officer material and who got to clean latrines.

Sure, intelligence matters. Some people are blessed with more of it than other people, and that makes certain things easier for them. Ditto for creative talent, or athletic prowess, or perfect pitch, or any of life's other precious gifts. But this raw talent is really only half the total picture. The other half we must paint for ourselves.

Even the people at the Educational Testing Service, the New Jersey company that administers many of today's standardized tests, now go to great lengths to emphasize how incomplete their results really are. School admissions officers are warned not to interpret these results too rigidly. A whole range of other factors must apply—personal enthusiasm at the top of the list.

National Hockey League Hall-of-Famer Denis Potvin, who led the New York Islanders to four straight Stanley Cups, knows a little something about enthusiasm.

"When I got to training camp," the former Islanders captain remembered, "I needed to be emotionally excited about hockey. So I didn't take the approach that some players did, thinking I should skate all summer long. I actually felt the opposite: I didn't want to skate a lot.

"So when I got into training camp, I was never in as great shape physically as a lot of the people were. I knew I had to work extra hard to be in shape. But the thing I had over them was that I was genuinely enthusiastic about playing hockey again. Here it was, the fifteenth September of my professional career, and I felt like I was a kid again."

No, you can't fake enthusiasm. But yes—absolutely, yes—you can create it, you can nourish it, and you can put it to work for you. This is how I explain the process: "The way to acquire enthusiasm is to believe in what you are doing and in yourself and to want to get something definite accomplished. Enthusiasm will follow as night follows the day."

How can you get this process started? "By telling yourself what you like about what you are doing and passing on quickly from the part you don't like to the part you do like. Then act enthusiastic. Tell someone about it. Let them know why it interests you. If you act 'as if' you are interested in your job, that bit of acting will tend to make your interest real. It will also tend to decrease your fatigue, your tensions, and your worries."

Enthusiasm is easiest to attain when you have real goals in your life, things you are genuinely looking forward to. Let that happen, and enthusiasm will grow inside of you.

Wake up in the morning and take a minute to think about something pleasing that will happen that day. It doesn't have to be anything monumental. Maybe it's some part of your job you always enjoy. Maybe it's a friend you're meeting for lunch. Maybe it's a family outing, a beer with your friends, an hour on the squash court or in an aerobics class. Whatever the pleasing event is, what's important is this: life doesn't need to be dull or uninteresting. We all need goals and experiences worth looking forward to. These are the things that give a forward thrust to life. People who reflect on this even for a moment can build a whole new way of looking at life. They can break from the ruts that they're stuck in. They will, in other words, live enthusiastically. When you do, the results can be truly remarkable.

"Modern organizations need enthusiastic leadership more than ever," believes Andrés Navarro, president of Chile's SONDA, S.A. "That's almost a definition of leadership—the ability to transmit enthusiasm to other people for a common goal. If you want a group of people tomorrow or today to have enthusiasm and feel happy working on a project, it's useless to write a memo, 'Starting tomorrow everyone will have a lot of enthusiasm.'" You have to have the enthusiasm yourself.

"If you don't have enthusiasm, it's impossible you will transmit enthusiasm to anyone," Navarro says. "So if you want to change an environment, first of all you have got to change yourself. If you won't change first, you can't even change your children. If you want your son to be enthusiastic at playing soccer, you've got to be enthusiastic.

"Enthusiasm is something you transmit through your eyes, in the way you move, the way you act all day, more than the way you write it in a memo. Actually, I think all of us can have enthusiasm for something. If you don't feel any type of enthusiasm, you might as well be dead. Once you discover that you are enthusiastic in doing something, it's easy to develop the ability to get yourself enthusiastically behind almost any goal."

Indeed, having enthusiasm almost always assures success. That may be hard to believe, but the raw evidence suggests it is true.

You can tell that David Webb, the former president of Lever Brothers Company, brims with enthusiasm by just watching him walk through his office door. He's not a screamer or a grip-and-grin artist. But there's a positive, joyful spirit in his stride, head up, a look of eagerness in his eyes. This may sound trivial, but this look has more force than most of us imagine. This is no accident.

"People are always going to read you in the elevator," Webb says. "You express whatever your values are twenty-four hours a day. People have a good memory."

Webb goes on, "I learned this from a man who became the chairman of Unilever, Sir David Orr. I took over for him in India. He was the marketing director. He knew everyone. David

Orr went everywhere. We have a huge network of distributors. Every time you go to a distributor, they garland you. I toured all over India, and I tried desperately to find a distributor where David Orr hadn't been, where there wasn't some photograph of him on the wall. He knew every salesman in the country." It was Sir David's enthusiasm they all remembered.

Webb learned this lesson, and he didn't forget it as he rose through the ranks to CEO of Lever Brothers. "I'd met every salesman in this company—I think we've got about seven hundred fifty—within three months of being in the business," he recalls. "They know me. They can relate to me. I'm out there playing the fool with them sometimes, enjoying the fun, just being with them. I love the salesmen and the people in the plants. But there isn't anyone I don't like."

Thomas Doherty was an executive at Norstar Bank when the regional financial institution was acquired by Fleet Financial Group, Inc. Doherty stayed on, running all of Fleet's business for the New York City region.

Not surprisingly, many of Doherty's colleagues were extremely nervous about the change in ownership. "That's natural," Doherty says. "Customers, families, and friends are going to ask us, 'How do you feel about the merger?' If you're enthusiastic over it, then they are going to be enthusiastic. I think attitude and enthusiasm are what people are looking for. If you come to your desk every day and you have a long face, people read that immediately. But if you get on the elevator and you say good morning to everyone just as you have in the past, people notice that. They think, Gee, he's enthusiastic. Why not give it a chance?"

This prescription, of course, presupposes that there is something you like about your work. Assessing this realistically may require a little soul-searching. The truth of the matter is that there are things to like about most jobs, but let's not gloss over the hard reality: there are some jobs that are simply miserable—or simply inappropriate to your temperament, your skills, or your goals. If that condition applies to you, do something about it. You will never achieve real success if you cannot be excited by your life or your work. Many people have bounced around from job to job before finding the happy fit. There's nothing shameful about this. The shameful thing is to feel miserable about a job—and not try to make it better or find another one.

If you're feeling bored with life, the people around you will be falling asleep as well. If you're sarcastic and antagonistic, they will be too. If you're lukewarm, they will never boil.

So be enthusiastic. Watch the impact that has on the people around you, They'll grow more productive and eager to follow you. Passions, remember, are more powerful than cold ideas. And genuine enthusiasm is contagious.

NEVER UNDERESTIMATE
THE POWER OF ENTHUSIASM.

Points to Remember

1. Being louder doesn't make you seem more enthusiastic.
2. Enthusiasm is as crucial as hard work to succeed at a workplace.
3. You can help other people be more productive by opting for a positive attitude.

13

GROWING A VOCABULARY

"Only knowledge that is used sticks in your mind."

The term 'vocabulary' has a special as well as a general meaning. True, all vocabularies are grounded in the everyday words of the language, out of which grow the special vocabularies, but each such specialized group possesses a number of words of peculiar value for its own objects. These words may be used in other vocabularies also, but the fact that they are suited to a unique order of expression marks them as of special value to a particular craft or calling.

In this respect the public speaker differs not at all from the poet, the novelist, the scientist, the traveler. He must add to his everyday stock, words of value for the public presentation of thought. 'A study of the discourses of effective orators discloses the fact that they have a fondness for words signifying power, largeness, speed, action, color, light, and all their opposites. They frequently employ words expressive of the various emotions. Descriptive words, adjectives used in fresh relations with nouns, and apt epithets are freely employed. Indeed, the nature of public speech permits the use of mildly exaggerated words which, by the time they have reached the hearer's judgment, will leave only a just impression.'

FORM THE BOOK-NOTE HABIT

To possess a word involves three things: To know its special and broader meanings, to know its relation to other words, and to be able to use it. When you see or hear a familiar word used in an unfamiliar sense, jot it down, look it up, and master it. We have in mind a speaker of superior attainments who acquired his vocabulary by noting all new words he heard or read. These he mastered and put into use. Soon his vocabulary became large, varied, and exact. Use a new word accurately five times and it is yours. Professor Albert E. Hancock says: 'An author's vocabulary is of two kinds, latent and dynamic: latent—those words he understands; dynamic—those he can readily use. Every intelligent man knows all the words he needs, but he may not have them all ready for active service. The problem of literary diction consists in turning the latent into the dynamic.' Your dynamic vocabulary is the one you must especially cultivate.

In his essay on "A College Magazine" in the volume, *Memories and Portraits*, Stevenson shows how he rose from imitation to originality in the use of words. He had particular reference to the formation of his literary style, but words are the raw materials of style, and his excellent example may well be followed judiciously by the public speaker. Words in their relations are vastly more important than words considered singly.

Whenever I read a book or a passage that particularly pleased me, in which a thing was said or an effect rendered with propriety, in which there was either some conspicuous force or some happy distinction in the style, I must sit down at once and set myself to ape that quality. I was unsuccessful, and I knew it; and tried again, and was again unsuccessful, and always unsuccessful; but at least in these vain bouts I got some practice in rhythm, in harmony, in construction and coordination of parts.

I have thus played the sedulous ape to Hazlitt, to Lamb, to Wordsworth, to Sir Thomas Browne, to Defoe, to Hawthorne, to Montaigne.

That, like it or not, is the way to learn to write; whether I have profited or not, that is the way. It was the way Keats learned, and there never was a finer temperament for literature than Keats'.

It is the great point of these imitations that there still shines beyond the student's reach, his inimitable model. Let him try as he please, he is still sure of failure; and it is an old and very true saying that failure is the only highroad to success.

FORM THE REFERENCE-BOOK HABIT

Do not be content with your general knowledge of a word—press your study until you have mastered its individual shades of meaning and usage. Mere fluency is sure to become despicable, but accuracy never. The dictionary contains the crystallized usage of intellectual giants. No one who would write effectively dare despise its definitions and discriminations. Think, for example, of the different meanings of mantle, or model, or quantity. Any late edition of an unabridged dictionary is good, and is worth making sacrifices to own.

Books of synonyms and antonyms—used cautiously, for there are few perfect synonyms in any language—will be found of great help. Consider the shades of meanings among such word-groups as thief, peculator, defaulter, embezzler, burglar, yeggman, robber, bandit, marauder, pirate, and many more; or the distinctions among Hebrew, Jew, Israelite and Semite. Remember that no book of synonyms is trustworthy unless used with a dictionary. *A Thesaurus of the English Language*, by Dr. Francis A. March, is expensive, but full and authoritative. Of smaller books of synonyms and antonyms there are plenty.

Study the connectives of English speech. Fernald's book on this title is a mine of gems. Unsuspected pitfalls lie in the loose use of and, or, for, while, and a score of tricky little connectives.

Word derivations are rich in suggestiveness. Our English owes so much to foreign tongues and has changed so much with the centuries that whole addresses may grow out of a single root-idea hidden away in an ancient word-origin. Translation, also, is excellent exercise in word-mastery and consorts well with the study of derivations.

Phrase books that show the origins of familiar expressions will surprise most of us by showing how carelessly everyday speech is used. Brewer's *A Dictionary of Phrase, and Fable*, Edwards' *Words, Facts, and Phrases*, and Thornton's *An American Glossary*, are all good—the last, an expensive work in three volumes.

A prefix or a suffix may essentially change the force of the stem, as in master-ful and master-ly, contempt-ible and contempt-uous, envi-ous and envi-able. Thus to study words in groups, according to their stems, prefixes, and suffixes is to gain a mastery over their shades of meaning, and introduce us to other related words.

DO NOT FAVOUR ONE SET OR KIND OF WORDS MORE THAN ANOTHER

"Sixty years and more ago, Lord Brougham, addressing the students of the University of Glasgow, laid down the rule that the native (Anglo-Saxon) part of our vocabulary was to be favored at the expense of that other part which has come from the Latin and Greek. The rule was an impossible one, and Lord Brougham himself never tried seriously to observe it; nor, in truth, has any great writer made the attempt. Not only is our language highly composite, but the component words have, in De Quincey's phrase, 'happily coalesced.' It is easy to jest at words in -osity and -ation, as 'dictionary' words, and the like. But even Lord Brougham would have found it difficult to dispense with pomposity and imagination."

The short, vigorous Anglo-Saxon will always be preferred for passages of special thrust and force, just as the Latin will continue to furnish us with flowing and smooth expressions; to mingle all sorts, however, will give variety—and that is most to be desired.

DISCUSS WORDS WITH THOSE WHO KNOW THEM

Since the language of the platform follows closely the diction of everyday speech, many useful words may be acquired in conversation with cultivated men, and when such discussion takes the form of disputation as to the meanings and usages of words, it will prove doubly valuable. The development of word-power marches with the growth of individuality.

SEARCH FAITHFULLY FOR THE RIGHT WORD

Books of reference are tripled in value when their owner has a passion for getting the kernels out of their shells. Ten minutes a day will do wonders for the nut-cracker.

> "I am growing so peevish about my writing," says Flaubert, "I am like a man whose ear is true, but who plays falsely on the violin: his fingers refuse to reproduce

precisely those sounds of which he has the inward sense. Then the tears come rolling down from the poor scraper's eyes and the bow falls from his hand."

The same brilliant Frenchman sent this sound advice to his pupil, Guy de Maupassant: "Whatever may be the thing which one wishes to say, there is but one word for expressing it, only one verb to animate it, only one adjective to qualify it. It is essential to search for this word, for this verb, for this adjective, until they are discovered, and to be satisfied with nothing else."

Walter Savage Landor once wrote: "I hate false words, and seek with care, difficulty, and moroseness those that fit the thing."

Points to Remember

1. Form a habit of jotting down unfamiliar words that you hear or read to expand your vocabulary.
2. Research on the origin of the words to gain more expertise.
3. Most effective way to inculcate new words in your speech is by using them while conversing with other people.

14

TALK ABOUT YOUR OWN MISTAKES FIRST

"Instead of condemning people, let's try to understand them. Let's try to figure out why they do what they do. That's a lot more profitable and intriguing than criticism; and it breeds sympathy, tolerance and kindness. To know all is to forgive all."

My niece, Josephine Carnegie, had come to New York to be my secretary. She was nineteen, had graduated from high school three years previously, and her business experience was a trifle more than zero. She became one of the most proficient secretaries west of Suez, but in the beginning, she was—well, susceptible to improvement. One day when I started to criticize her, I said to myself: "Just a minute, Dale Carnegie; just a minute. You are twice as old as Josephine. You have ten thousand times as much business experience. How can you possibly expect her to have your viewpoint, your judgment, your initiative—mediocre though they may be? And just a minute, Dale, what were you doing at nineteen? Remember the asinine mistakes and blunders you made? Remember the time you did this…and that…?"

After thinking the matter over, honestly and impartially, I concluded that Josephine's batting average at nineteen was better than mine had been—and that, I'm sorry to confess, isn't paying Josephine much of a compliment.

So after that, when I wanted to call Josephine's attention to a mistake, I used to begin by saying, "You have made a mistake, Josephine, but the Lord knows, it's no worse than many I have made. You were not born with judgment. That comes only with experience, and you are better than I was at your age. I have been guilty of so many stupid, silly things myself, I have very little inclination to criticize you or anyone. But don't you think it would have been wiser if you had done so and so?"

It isn't nearly so difficult to listen to a recital of your faults if the person criticizing begins by humbly admitting that he, too, is far from impeccable.

E. G. Dillistone, an engineer in Brandon, Manitoba, Canada, was having problems with his new secretary. Letters he dictated were coming to his desk for signature with two or three spelling mistakes per page. Mr. Dillistone reported how he handled this:

"Like many engineers, I have not been noted for my excellent English or spelling. For years I have kept a little black thumb-index book for words I had trouble spelling. When it became apparent that merely pointing out the errors was not going to cause my secretary to do more proofreading and dictionary work, I resolved to take another approach. When the next letter came to my attention that had errors in it, I sat down with the typist and said:

"'Somehow this word doesn't look right. It's one of the words I always have had trouble with. That's the reason I started this spelling book of mine. (I opened the book to the appropriate page.) Yes, here it is. I'm very conscious of the spelling now because people do judge us by our letters, and misspellings make us look less professional.'

"I don't know whether she copied my system or not, but since that conversation, her frequency of spelling errors has been significantly reduced."

The polished Prince Bernhard von Bülow learned the sharp necessity of doing this back in 1909. Von Bülow was then the imperial chancellor of Germany, and on the throne sat Wilhelm II—Wilhelm, the haughty; Wilhelm, the arrogant; Wilhelm, the last of the German kaisers, building an army and navy that he boasted could whip their weight in wildcats.

Then an astonishing thing happened. The kaiser said things, incredible things, things that rocked the continent and started a series of explosions heard around the world. To make matters worse, the kaiser made silly, egotistical, absurd announcements in public. He made them while he was a guest in England, and he gave his royal permission to have them printed in the *Daily Telegraph*. For example, he declared that he was the only German who felt friendly toward the English; that he was constructing a navy against the menace of Japan; that he, and he alone, had saved England from being humbled in the dust by Russia and France; that it had been *his* campaign plan that enabled England's Lord Roberts to defeat the Boers in South Africa; and so on and on.

No other such amazing words had ever fallen from the lips of a European king in peacetime within a hundred years. The entire continent buzzed with the fury of a hornet's nest. England was incensed. German statesmen were aghast. And in the midst of all this consternation, the kaiser became panicky and suggested to Prince von Bülow, the imperial chancellor, that he take the blame. Yes, he wanted von Bülow to announce that it was all his responsibility, that he had advised his monarch to say these incredible things.

"But Your Majesty," von Bülow protested, "it seems to me utterly impossible that anybody either in Germany or England could suppose me capable of having advised Your Majesty to say any such thing."

The moment those words were out of von Bülow's mouth, he realized he had made a grave mistake. The Kaiser blew up.

"You consider me a donkey," he shouted, "capable of blunders you yourself could never have committed."

Von Bülow knew that he ought to have praised before he condemned; but since it was too late, he did the next best thing. He praised after he had criticized. And it worked a miracle.

"I'm far from suggesting that," he answered respectfully. "Your Majesty surpasses me in many respects; not only, of course, in naval and military knowledge, but above all, in natural science. I have often listened in admiration when Your Majesty explained the barometer, or wireless telegraphy, or the Roentgen rays. I am shamefully ignorant of all branches of natural science, have no notion of chemistry or physics, and am quite incapable of explaining the simplest of natural phenomena. But," von Bülow continued, "in compensation, I possess some historical knowledge and perhaps certain qualities useful in politics, especially in diplomacy."

The kaiser beamed. Von Bülow had praised him. Von Bülow had exalted him and humbled himself. The kaiser could forgive anything after that. "Haven't I always told you," he exclaimed with enthusiasm, "that we complete one another famously? We should stick together, and we will!"

He shook hands with von Bülow, not once, but several times. And later in the day he waxed so enthusiastic that he exclaimed with doubled fists, "If anyone says anything to me against Prince von Bülow, *I shall punch him in the nose.*"

Von Bülow saved himself in time—but, canny diplomat that he was, he nevertheless had made one error: he should have *begun* by talking about his own shortcomings and Wilhelm's superiority—not by intimating that the kaiser was a half-wit in need of a guardian.

If a few sentences humbling oneself and praising the other party can turn a haughty, insulted kaiser into a staunch friend, imagine what humility and praise can do for you and me in our daily contacts. Rightly used, they will work veritable miracles in human relations.

Admitting one's own mistakes—even when one hasn't corrected them—can help convince somebody to change his or her behavior. This was illustrated more recently by Clarence Zerhusen of Timonium, Maryland, when he discovered his fifteen-year-old son was experimenting with cigarettes.

"Naturally, I didn't want David to smoke," Mr. Zerhusen told us, "but his mother and I smoked cigarettes; we were giving him a bad example all the time. I explained to Dave how I started smoking at about his age and how the nicotine had gotten the best of me and now it was nearly impossible for me to stop. I reminded him how irritating my cough was and how he had been after me to give up cigarettes not many years before. I didn't exhort him to stop or make threats or warn him about their dangers. All I did was point out how I was hooked on cigarettes and what it had meant to me.

"He thought about it for a while and decided he wouldn't smoke until he had graduated from high school. As the years went by David never did start smoking and has no intention of ever doing so.

"As a result of that conversation I made the decision to stop smoking myself, and with the support of my family, I have succeeded."

Points to Remember

1. To be able to criticize and not be hated for it, speak about your mistakes first.
2. Good leadership is to correct your subordinates without lowering their morale.
3. Sharing responsibility with others for their errors strengthens relationships.

15

HOW FAMOUS SPEAKERS PREPARED THEIR ADDRESSES

"Pay less attention to what men say. Just watch what they do."

No sane man would start to build a house without some sort of plan, but why will he begin to deliver a speech without the vaguest kind of outline or programme?

A speech is a voyage with a purpose, and it must be charted. The man who starts nowhere, generally gets there.

I wish that I could paint this saying of Napoleon's in flaming letters of red a foot high over every doorway on the globe where students of public speaking foregather: "The art of war is a science in which nothing succeeds which has not been calculated and thought out."

That is just as true of speaking as of shooting. But do speakers realize it, or, if they do, do they always act on it? They do not. Most emphatically they do not. Many a talk has just a trifle more plan and arrangement than a bowl of Irish stew.

What is the best and most effective arrangement for a given set of ideas? No one can say until he has studied them. It is always a new problem, an eternal question that every speaker must ask and answer himself again and again.

SECRETS OF GREAT SPEAKERS

Woodrow Wilson

"I begin," said Woodrow Wilson when asked to explain his methods, "with a list of the topics I want to cover, *arranging them in my mind in their natural relations*—that is, I fit the bones of the thing together; then I write it out in shorthand. I have always been accustomed to writing in shorthand, finding it a great saver of time. This done, I copy it on my own typewriter, changing phrases, correcting sentences, and adding material as I go along."

Theodore Roosevelt

Theodore Roosevelt prepared his talks in the characteristic Rooseveltian manner: he dug all the facts, reviewed them, appraised them, determined their findings, arrived at his conclusions, arrived with a feeling of certainty that was unshakable.

Then, with a pad of notes before him, he started dictating and he dictated his speech very rapidly so that it would have rush and spontaneity and the spirit of life. Then he went over this typewritten copy, revised it, inserted, deleted, filled it with pencil marks, and then dictated it all over again. "I never won anything," said he, "without hard labor and the exercise of my best judgment and careful planning and working long in advance."

Often he called in critics to listen to him as he dictated or read his speech to them. He refused to debate with them the wisdom of what he had said. His mind was already made up on that point, and made up irrevocably. He wanted to be told, not what to say, but how to say it. Again and again he went over his typewritten copies, cutting, correcting, improving. That was the speech that the newspapers printed. Of course, he did not memorize it. He spoke extemporaneously. So the talk he actually delivered often differed somewhat from the published and polished one. But the task of dictating and revising was excellent preparation. It made him familiar with his material, with the order of his points. It gave him a smoothness and sureness and polish that he could hardly have obtained in any other fashion.

Sir Oliver Lodge

Sir Oliver Lodge told me that dictating his talks—dictating them rapidly and with substance, dictating them just as if he were actually talking to an audience—he had discovered to be an excellent means of preparation and practice.

Many of the students of this course have found it illuminating to dictate their talks to the dictaphone, and then to listen to themselves. Illuminating? Yes, and sometimes disillusioning and chastening also, I fear. It is a most wholesome exercise. I recommend it.

This practice of actually writing out what you are going to say will force you to think. It will clarify your ideas. It will hook them in your memory. It will reduce your mental wandering to a minimum. It will improve your diction.

Benjamin Franklin

Benjamin Franklin tells in his *Autobiography* how he improved his diction, how he developed readiness in using words and how he taught himself method in arranging his thoughts. This story of his life is a literary classic and, unlike most classics, it is easy to read and thoroughly enjoyable. It is almost a model of plain, straightforward English. Every businessman can peruse it with pleasure and profit. I think you will like the selection I refer to; here it is:

> About this time I met with an odd volume of the *Spectator*. It was the third. I had never before seen any of them. I bought it, read it over and over and was much delighted with it. I thought the writing excellent, and wished, if possible, to imitate it. With this view I took some of the papers, and, making short hints of the sentiment in each sentence laid them by a few days, and then, without looking at the book, try'd to complete the papers again, by expressing each hinted sentiment at length, and as fully as it had been expressed before, in any suitable words that should come to hand. Then I compared my *Spectator* with the original, discovered some of my faults and corrected them. But I found a stock of words, and a readiness in recollecting and using them, which I thought I should have acquired before that time if I had gone on making verses; since the continual occasion for words of the same import, but of different length, to suit the measure, or of different sounds for the rhyme, would have laid me under a constant necessity of searching for variety, and also have tended to fix that variety in my mind, and make me master of it. Therefore I took some of the tales and turned them back again. I also sometimes jumbled my collections of hints into confusion, and after some weeks endeavoured to reduce them into the best order, before I began to form the full sentences and complete the paper. *This was to teach me method in the arrangement of thoughts.* By comparing my work afterwards with the original, I discovered many

faults and amended them; but I sometimes had the pleasure of fancying that, in certain particulars of small import, I had been lucky enough to improve the method of the language, and this encouraged me to think I might possibly in time come to be a tolerable English writer, of which I was extremely ambitious.

Points to Remember

1. Multiple methods to prepare speech by great speakers.
2. Writing down your speech helps you to memorize it better.
3. Accepting healthy criticism can be a good way to improve yourself as a speaker.

16

HOW TO MAKE YOUR MEANING CLEAR

"The gun that scatters too much does not bag the birds."

A famous English bishop, during the last war, spoke to some unlettered negro troops. They were on their way to the trenches; but a very small percentage of them had any adequate idea why they were being sent. I know: I questioned them. Yet the Lord Bishop talked to these negroes about "international amity" and "Servia's right to a place in the sun". Why, the half of those negroes did not know whether Servia was a town or a disease. He might as well, as far as results were concerned, have delivered a sonorous eulogy on the Nebular Hypothesis. However, not a single trooper left the hall while he was speaking: the military police with revolvers were stationed at every exit to prevent that consummation.

I do not wish to belittle the bishop. He is every inch a scholar, and before a body of collegiate men he would probably have been powerful, but he failed with these negroes, and he failed utterly: he did not know his audience, and he evidently knew neither the precise purpose of his talk nor how to accomplish it.

What do we mean by the purpose of an address? Just this: every talk, regardless of whether the speaker realizes it or not, has one of four major goals. What are they?

1. To make something clear.
2. To impress and convince.
3. To get action.
4. To entertain.

Let us illustrate these by a series of concrete examples.

Lincoln, who was always more or less interested in mechanics, once invented and patented a device for lifting stranded boats off sand bars and other obstructions. He worked in a mechanic's shop near his law office, making a model of his apparatus. Although the device finally came to naught, he was decidedly enthusiastic over its possibilities. When friends came to his office to view the model, he took no end of pains to explain it. The main purpose of those explanations was clearness.

When he delivered his immortal oration at Gettysburg, when he gave his first and second inaugural addresses, when Henry Clay died and Lincoln delivered an eulogy on his life—on all these occasions, Lincoln's main purpose was impressiveness and conviction. He had to be clear, of course, because he could be convincing; but, in these instances, clearness was not his major consideration.

In his talks to juries, he tried to win favorable decisions. In his political talks, he tried to win votes. His purpose, then, was *action*.

Two years before he was elected President, Lincoln prepared a lecture on Inventions. His purpose was entertainment. At least, that should have been his goal, but he was evidently not very successful in attaining it. His career as a popular lecturer was, in fact, a distinct disappointment. In one town, not a person came to hear him.

But he did succeed and he succeeded famously in the other

speeches of his that I have referred to. And why? Because, in those instances, he knew his goal, and he knew how to achieve it. He knew where he wanted to go and how to get there. And because so many speakers don't know just that, they often flounder and come to grief.

For example: I once saw a United States Congressman hooted and hissed and forced to leave the stage of the old New York Hippodrome, because he had—unconsciously, no doubt, but nevertheless, unwisely—chosen clearness as his goal. It was during the last war. He talked to his audience about how the United States was preparing. The crowd did not want to be instructed. They wanted to be entertained. They listened to him patiently, politely, for ten minutes, a quarter of an hour, hoping the performance would come to a rapid end. But it didn't. He rambled on and on; patience snapped and the audience would not stand for more. Someone began to cheer ironically. Others took it up. In a moment, a thousand people were whistling and shouting. The speaker, obtuse and incapable as he was of sensing the temper of his audience, had the bad taste to continue. That aroused them. A battle was on. Their impatience mounted to ire. They determined to silence him. Louder and louder grew their storm of protest. Finally, the roar of it, the anger of it drowned his words—he could not have been heard twenty feet away. So he was forced to give up, acknowledge defeat, and retire in humiliation.

Profit by his example. Know your goal. Choose it wisely before you set out to prepare your talk. Know how to reach it. Then set about it, doing it skilfully and with science.

All this requires knowledge, special and technical instruction.

AVOID TECHNICAL TERMS

If you belong to a profession the work of which is technical—if you are a lawyer, a physician, an engineer, or are in a highly specialized line of business—be doubly careful when you talk to outsiders, to express yourself in plain terms and to give necessary details.

I say be doubly careful for, as a part of my professional duties, I have listened to hundreds of speeches that failed right at this point and failed woefully. The speakers appeared totally unconscious of the general public's widespread and profound ignorance regarding their particular specialties. So what happened? They rambled on and on, uttering thoughts, using phrases that fitted into their experience and were instantly and continuously meaningful to them; but to the uninitiated, they were about as clear as a river after the rains have fallen on the newly-ploughed cornfields along its banks.

What should such a speaker do? He ought to read and heed the following advice from the facile pen of ex-Senator Beveridge:

> It is a good practice to pick out the least intelligent looking person in the audience and strive to make that person interested in your argument. This can be done only by lucid statement of fact and clear reasoning. An even better method is to centre your talk on some small boy or girl present with parents.
>
> Say to yourself—say out loud to your audience, if you like—that you will try to be so plain that the child will understand and remember your explanation of the question discussed, and after the meeting be able to tell what you have said.

THE SECRET TO LINCOLN'S CLEARNESS

Lincoln had a deep and abiding affection for putting a proposition so that it would be instantly clear to everyone. In his first message to Congress, he used the phrase "sugar-coated". Mr. Defrees, the public printer, being Lincoln's personal friend, suggested to him that although the phrase might be all right for a stump speech in Illinois, it was not dignified enough for a historical state paper. "Well, Defrees," Lincoln replied, "if you think the time will ever come when the people will not understand what 'sugar-coated' means, I'll alter it; otherwise, I think I'll let it go."

He once explained to Dr. Gulliver, the President of Knox College, how he developed his "passion" for plain language, as he phrased it:

> Among my earliest recollections I remember how, when a mere child. I used to get irritated when anybody talked to me in a way I could not understand. I don't think I ever got angry at anything else in my life. But that always disturbed my temper, and has ever since. I can remember going to my little bedroom, after hearing the neighbors talk of an evening with my father, and spending no small part of the night walking up and down and trying to make out the exact meaning of some of their, to me, dark sayings. I could not sleep, though I often tried to, when I got on such a hunt after an idea, until I had caught it, and when I thought I had got it I was not satisfied until I had repeated it over and over, until I had put it in language plain enough as I thought for any boy I knew to comprehend. This was a kind of passion with me, and it has since stuck by me.

A passion? Yes, it must have amounted to that, for Mentor Graham, the schoolmaster of New Salem, testified: "I have known Lincoln to study for hours the best way of three to express an idea."

An all too common reason why men fail to be intelligible is this: the thing they wish to express is not clear even to themselves. Hazy impressions! Indistinct, vague ideas! The result? Their minds work no better in a mental fog than a camera does in a physical fog. They need to be as disturbed over obscurity and ambiguity as Lincoln was. They need to use his methods.

Points to Remember

1. Know your audience.
2. Use plain language to avoid technical jargons.
3. Identify your goal as a speaker and stick to it.

17

RIGHT THINKING AND PERSONALITY

> *"Remember happiness doesn't depend upon who you are or what you have; it depends solely on what you think."*

The speaker's most valuable possession is personality—that indefinable, imponderable something which sums up what we are, and makes us different from others; that distinctive force of self which operates appreciably on those whose lives we touch. It is personality alone that makes us long for higher things. Rob us of our sense of individual life, with its gains and losses, its duties and joys, and we grovel. Says John Stuart Mill,

> Few human creatures, "would consent to be changed into any of the lower animals for a promise of the fullest allowance of a beast's pleasures; no intelligent human being would consent to be a fool, no instructed person would be an ignoramus, no person of feeling and conscience would be selfish and base, even though he should be persuaded that the fool, or the dunce, or the rascal is better satisfied with his lot than they with theirs... It is better to be a human being dissatisfied than a pig satisfied, better to be a Socrates dissatisfied than a fool satisfied. And if the fool or the pig is of a different

> opinion, it is only because they know only their own side of the question. The other party to the comparison knows both sides."

Now it is precisely because the Socrates type of person lives on the plane of right thinking and restrained feeling and willing, that he prefers his state to that of the animal. All that a man is, all his happiness, his sorrow, his achievements, his failures, his magnetism, his weakness, all are in an amazingly large measure the direct results of his thinking. Thought and heart combine to produce right thinking: "As a man thinketh in his heart so is he." As he does not think in his heart so he can never become.

Since this is true, personality can be developed and its latent powers brought out by careful cultivation. We have long since ceased to believe that we are living in a realm of chance. So clear and exact are nature's laws that we forecast, scores of years in advance, the appearance of a certain comet and foretell to the minute an eclipse of the sun. And we understand this law of cause and effect in all our material realms. We do not plant potatoes and expect to pluck hyacinths. The law is universal: it applies to our mental powers, to morality, to personality, quite as much as to the heavenly bodies and the grain of the fields. 'Whatsoever a man soweth that shall he also reap,' and nothing else.

Character has always been regarded as one of the chief factors of the speaker's power. Cato defined the orator as *vir bonus dicendi peritus*—a good man skilled in speaking. Phillips Brooks says: "Nobody can truly stand as a utterer before the world, unless he be profoundly living and earnestly thinking." Emerson says:

> Character is a natural power like light and heat, and all nature cooperates with it. The reason why we feel one

man's presence, and do not feel another's is as simple as gravity. Truth is the summit of being: justice is the application of it to affairs. All individual natures stand in a scale, according to the purity of this element in them. The will of the pure runs down into other natures, as water runs down from a higher into a lower vessel. This natural force is no more to be withstood than any other natural force... Character is nature in the highest form.

WATER YOUR MIND

It is absolutely impossible for impure, bestial and selfish thoughts to blossom into loving and altruistic habits. Thistle seeds bring forth only the thistle. Contrariwise, it is entirely impossible for continual altruistic, sympathetic, and serviceful thoughts to bring forth a low and vicious character. Either thoughts or feelings precede and determine all our actions. Actions develop into habits, habits constitute character, and character determines destiny. Therefore to guard our thoughts and control our feelings is to shape our destinies. The syllogism is complete, and old as it is it is, still true.

Since "character is nature in the highest form," the development of character must proceed on natural lines. The garden left to itself will bring forth weeds and scrawny plants, but the flower-beds nurtured carefully will blossom into fragrance and beauty.

As the student entering college largely determines his vocation by choosing from the different courses of the curriculum, so do we choose our characters by choosing our thoughts. We are steadily going up toward that which we most wish for, or steadily sinking to the level of our low desires. What we secretly cherish in our hearts is a symbol of what we shall receive. Our trains of thoughts are hurrying us on to our destiny. When you see the flag fluttering to the South, you know the wind is coming from the North. When you see the straws and papers being carried to the Northward you realize the wind is blowing out of the South. It is just as easy to ascertain a man's thoughts by observing the tendency of his character.

Let it not be suspected for one moment that all this is merely a preachment on the question of morals. It is that, but much more, for it touches the whole man—his imaginative nature, his ability to control his feelings, the mastery of his thinking faculties, and—perhaps most largely—his power to will and to carry his volitions into effective action.

Right thinking constantly assumes that the will sits enthroned to execute the dictates of mind, conscience and heart. Never tolerate for an instant the suggestion that your will is not absolutely efficient. The way to will is to will—and the very first time you are tempted to break a worthy resolution—and you will be, you may be certain of that—make your fight then and there. You cannot afford to lose that fight. You must win it—don't swerve for an instant, but keep that resolution if it kills you. It will not, but you must fight just as though life depended on the victory; and indeed your personality may actually lie in the balances!

Your success or failure as a speaker will be determined very largely by your thoughts and your mental attitude. The present writer had a student of limited education enter one of his classes in public speaking. He proved to be a very poor speaker; and the instructor could conscientiously do little but point out faults. However, the young man was warned not to be discouraged. With sorrow in his voice and the essence of earnestness beaming from his eyes, he replied: "I will not be discouraged! I want so badly to know how to speak!" It was warm, human, and from the very heart. And he did keep on trying—and developed into a creditable speaker.

There is no power under the stars that can defeat a man with that attitude. He who down in the deeps of his heart earnestly longs to get facility in speaking, and is willing to make the sacrifices necessary, will reach his goal. "Ask and ye shall receive; seek and ye shall find; knock and it shall be opened unto you," is indeed applicable to those who would acquire speech-power. You will not realize the prize that you wish for languidly, but the goal that you start out to attain with the spirit of the old guard that dies but never surrenders, you will surely reach.

Your belief in your ability and your willingness to make sacrifices for that belief, are the double index to your future achievements. Lincoln had a dream of his possibilities as a speaker. He transmuted that dream into life solely because he walked many miles to borrow books which he read by the log-fire glow at night. He sacrificed much to realize his vision. Livingstone had a great faith in his ability to serve the benighted races of Africa. To actualize that faith he gave up all. Leaving England for the interior of the Dark Continent he struck the death blow to Europe's profits from the slave trade. Joan of Arc had great self-confidence, glorified by an infinite capacity for sacrifice. She drove the English beyond the Loire, and stood beside Charles while he was crowned.

These all realized their strongest desires. The law is universal. Desire greatly, and you shall achieve; sacrifice much, and you shall obtain.

Stanton Davis Kirkham has beautifully expressed this thought:

You may be keeping accounts, and presently you shall walk out of the door that has for so long seemed to you the barrier of your ideals, and shall find yourself before an audience—the pen still behind your ear, the ink stains on your fingers—and then and there shall pour out the torrent of your inspiration. You may be driving sheep, and you shall wander to the city—bucolic and open-mouthed; shall wander under the intrepid guidance of the spirit into the studio of the master, and after a time he shall say, 'I have nothing more to teach you.' And now you have become the master, who did so recently dream of great things while driving sheep. You shall lay down the saw and the plane to take upon yourself the regeneration of the world.

Points to Remember

1. It is your personality that makes you a leader and not a follower, so nurture it.
2. Right thinking and strong will are required to abstain from temptations.
3. You cannot obtain anything without sacrificing something.

18

THE TALK TO CONVINCE

"Why talk about what we want? That is childish. Absurd. Of course, you are interested in what you want. You are eternally interested in it. But no one else is. The rest of us are just like you: we are interested in what we want."

Quintilian described the orator as "a good man skilled in speaking." He was talking about sincerity and character. Nothing said in this book, nor anything which will be said, can take the place of this essential attribute of speaking effectiveness. Pierpont Morgan said that character was the best way to obtain credit; it is also the best way to win the confidence of the audience.

"The sincerity with which a man speaks," said Alexander Woolcott, "imparts to his voice a color of truth no perjurer can feign."

Especially when the purpose of our talk is to convince, it is necessary to set forth our own ideas with the inner glow that comes from sincere conviction. We must first be convinced before we attempt to convince others.

GET A YES-RESPONSE

Walter Dill Scott, former president of Northwestern University, said that "every idea, concept, or conclusion which enters the mind is held as true unless hindered by some contradictory idea." That boils down to keeping the audience yes-minded. My good friend Professor Harry Overstreet brilliantly examined the psychological background of this concept in a lecture at the New School for Social Research in New York City:

> The skillful speaker gets at the outset a number of yes-responses. He has thereby set the psychological processes of his listeners moving in the affirmative direction. It is like the movement of a billiard ball. Propel it in one direction, and it takes some force to deflect it, far more force to send it back in the opposite direction.
>
> The psychological patterns here are quite clear.
>
> When a person says "No" and really means it, he is doing far more than saying a word of two letters. His entire organism—glandular, nervous, muscular—gathers itself together into a condition of rejection. There is, usually in minute but sometimes in observable degree, a physical withdrawal, or readiness for withdrawal. The whole neuromuscular system, in short, sets itself on guard against acceptance. Where, on the contrary, a person says "Yes," none of the withdrawing activities takes place. The organism is in a forward-moving, accepting, open attitude. Hence the more "Yesses" we can, at the very outset, induce, the more likely we are to succeed in capturing the attention for our ultimate proposal.
>
> It is a very simple technique—this yes-response. And yet how much neglected! It often seems as if people

get a sense of their own importance by antagonizing at the outset. The radical comes into a conference with his conservative brethren; and immediately he must make them furious! What, as a matter of fact, is the good of it? If he simply does it in order to get some pleasure out of it for himself, he may be pardoned. But if he expects to achieve something, he is only psychologically stupid.

Get a student to say "No" at the beginning, or a customer, child, husband, or wife, and it takes the wisdom and patience of angels to transform that bristling negative into an affirmative.

How is one going to get these desirable "yes-responses" at the very outset? Fairly simple. "My way of opening and winning an argument," confided Lincoln, "is to first find a common ground of agreement." Lincoln found it even when he was discussing the highly inflammable subject of slavery. "For the first half hour," declared *The Mirror,* a neutral paper reporting one of his talks, "his opponents would agree with every word he uttered. From that point he began to lead them off, little by little, until it seemed as if he had got them all into his fold."

Is it not evident that the speaker who argues with his audience is merely arousing their stubbornness, putting them on the defensive, making it well-nigh impossible for them to change their minds? Is it wise to start by saying, "I am going to prove so and so"? Aren't your hearers liable to accept that as a challenge and remark silently, "Let's see you do it"?

Is it not much more advantageous to begin by stressing something that you and all of your hearers believe, and then to raise some pertinent question that everyone would like to have answered? Then take your audience with you in an earnest search for the answer. While on that search, present the facts as you see them so clearly that they will be led to accept your conclusions as their own. They will have much more faith in some truth that they have discovered for themselves. "The best argument is that which seems merely an explanation."

In every controversy, no matter how wide and bitter the differences, there is always some common ground of agreement on which a speaker can invite everyone to meet. To illustrate: On February 3, 1960, the prime minister of Great Britain, Harold Macmillan, addressed both houses of the Parliament of the Union of South Africa. He had to present the United Kingdom's non-racial viewpoint before the legislature body at a time when apartheid was the prevailing policy. Did he begin his talk with this essential difference in outlook? No. He began by stressing the great economic progress made by South Africa, the significant contributions made by South Africa to the world. Then, with skill and tact he brought up the questions of differing viewpoints. Even here, he indicated that he was well aware that these differences were based on sincere conviction. His whole talk was a masterly statement reminding one of Lincoln's gentle but firm utterances in the years before Fort Sumter. "As a fellow member of the Commonwealth," said the Prime Minister, "it is our earnest desire to give South Africa our support and encouragement, but I hope you won't mind my saying frankly that there are some aspects of your policies which make it impossible for us to do this without being false to our deep convictions about the political destinies of free men to which in our own territories we are trying to give effect. I think we ought as friends to face together, without seeking to apportion credit or blame, the fact that in the world of today this difference of outlook lies between us."

No matter how determined one was to differ with a speaker,

a statement like that would tend to convince you of the speaker's fair-mindedness.

What would have been the result had Prime Minister Macmillan set out immediately to emphasize the difference in policy rather than the common ground of agreement? Professor James Harvey Robinson's enlightening book, *The Mind in the Making*, gives the psychological answer to that question:

> We sometimes find ourselves changing our minds without any resistance or heavy emotion, but if we are told we are wrong we resent the imputation and harden our hearts. We are incredibly heedless in the formation of our beliefs, but find ourselves filled with an illicit passion for them when anyone proposes to rob us of their companionship. It is obviously not the ideas themselves that are dear to us, but our self-esteem which is threatened... The little word *my* is the most important one in human affairs, and properly to reckon with it is the beginning of wisdom. It has the same force whether it is *my* dinner, *my* dog, and *my* house, or *my* faith, *my* country and *my* God. We not only resent the imputation that our watch is wrong, or our car shabby, but that our conception of the canals of Mars, of the pronunciation of "Epictetus," of the medicinal value of salicine, or of the date of Sargon I, are subject to revision... We like to continue to believe what we have been accustomed to accept as true, and the resentment aroused when doubt is cast upon any of our assumptions leads us to seek every manner of excuse for clinging to it. The result is that most of our so-called reasoning consists in finding arguments for going on believing as we already do.

SPEAK WITH CONTAGIOUS ENTHUSIASM

Contradicting ideas are much less likely to arise in the listener's mind when the speaker presents his ideas with feeling and contagious enthusiasm. I say "contagious," for enthusiasm is just that. It thrusts aside all negative and opposing ideas. When your aim is to convince, remember it is more productive to stir emotions than to arouse thoughts. Feelings are more powerful than cold ideas. To arouse feelings one must be intensely in earnest. Regardless of the petty phrases a man may concoct, regardless of the illustrations he may assemble, regardless of the harmony of his voice and the grace of his gestures, if he does not speak sincerely, these are hollow and glittering trappings. If you would impress an audience, be impressed yourself. Your spirit, shining through your eyes, radiating through your voice, and proclaiming itself through your manner, will communicate itself to your audience.

Every time you speak, and especially when your avowed purpose is to convince, what you do determines the attitude of your listeners. If you are lukewarm, so will they be; if you are flippant and antagonistic, so will they be. "When the congregation falls asleep," wrote Henry Ward Beecher, "there is only one thing to do; provide the usher with a sharp stick and have him prod the preacher."

I was once one of three judges called on to award the Curtis medal at Columbia University. There were half a dozen undergraduates, all of them elaborately trained, all of them eager to acquit themselves well. But—with only a single exception—what they were striving for was to win the medal. They had little or no desire to convince.

They had chosen their topics because these topics permitted oratorical development. They had no deep personal interest in the arguments they were making. And their successive talks were merely exercises in the art of delivery.

The exception was a Zulu Prince. He had selected as his theme "The Contribution of Africa to Modern Civilization." He put intense feeling into every word he uttered. His talk was no mere exercise; it was a living thing, born of conviction and enthusiasm. He spoke as the representative of his people, of his continent; with wisdom, high character, and good will, he brought us a message of his people's hopes and a plea for our understanding.

We gave him the medal although he was possibly no more accomplished in addressing a large group than two or three of his competitors. What we judges recognized was that his talk had the true fire of sincerity; it was ablaze with truth. Beside it, the other talks were only flickering gas-logs.

The Prince had learned in his own way in a distant land that you can't project your personality in a talk to others by using reason alone: you have to reveal to them how deeply you yourself believe in what you say.

SHOW RESPECT AND AFFECTION FOR YOUR AUDIENCE

"The human personality demands love and it also demands respect," Dr. Norman Vincent Peale said as a prelude to speaking of a professional comedian. "Every human being has an inner sense of worth, of importance, of dignity. Wound that and you have lost that person forever. So when you love and respect a person you build him up and, accordingly, he loves and esteems you.

"At one time I was on a program with an entertainer. I did not know the man well, but since that meeting I read that he was having difficulty, and I think I know why.

"I had been sitting beside him quietly for I was about to speak. 'You aren't nervous, are you?' he asked.

"'Why, yes,' I replied. 'I always get a little nervous before I stand up before an audience. I have a profound respect for an audience and the responsibility makes me a bit nervous. Don't you get nervous?'

"'No,' he said, 'Why should I? Audiences fall for anything. They are a lot of dopes.'

"'I don't agree with you,' I said. They are your sovereign judges. I have great respect for audiences.'"

When he read about this man's waning popularity Dr. Peale was sure the reason lay in an attitude that antagonized others instead of winning them.

What an object lesson for all of us who want to impart something to other people!

BEGIN IN A FRIENDLY WAY

An atheist once challenged William Paley to disprove his contention that there was no Supreme Being. Very quietly Paley took out his watch, opened the case, and said: "If I were to tell you that those levers and wheels and springs made themselves and fitted themselves together and started running on their own account, wouldn't you question my intelligence? Of course, you would. But look up at the stars. Every one of them has its perfect appointed course and motion—the earth and planets around the sun, and the whole group pitching along at more than a million miles a day. Each star is another sun with its own group of worlds, rushing on through space like our own solar system. Yet there are no collisions, no disturbance, no confusion. All quiet, efficient, and controlled. Is it easier to believe that they just happened or that someone made them so?"

Suppose he had retorted to his antagonist at the outset: "No God? Don't be a silly ass. You don't know what you are talking about." What would have happened? Doubtlessly a verbal joust—a wordy war would have ensued, as futile as it was fiery. The atheist would have risen with an unholy zeal upon him to fight for his opinions with all the fury of a wildcat. Why? Because, as Professor Overstreet has pointed out, they were *his* opinions, and his precious, indispensable self-esteem would have been threatened; his pride would have been at stake.

Since pride is such a fundamentally explosive characteristic of human nature, wouldn't it be the part of wisdom to get a man's pride working for us, instead of against us? How? By showing, as Paley did, that the thing we propose is very similar to something that our opponent already believes. That renders it easier for him to accept than to reject your proposal. That prevents contradictory and opposing ideas from arising in the mind to vitiate what we have said.

Paley showed delicate appreciation of how the human mind functions. Most men, however, lack this subtle ability to enter the citadel of a man's beliefs arm in arm with the owner. They erroneously imagine that in order to take the citadel, they must storm it, batter it down by a frontal attack. What happens? The moment hostilities commence, the drawbridge is lifted, the great gates are slammed and bolted, the mailed archers draw their long bows—the battle of words and wounds is on. Such frays always end in a draw; neither has convinced the other of anything.

This more sensible method I am advocating is not new. It was used long ago by Saint Paul. He employed it in that famous address of his to the Athenians on Mars Hill—employed it with an adroitness and finesse that compels our admiration across nineteen centuries. He was a man of finished education;

and, after his conversion to Christianity, his eloquence made him its leading advocate. One day he arrived at Athens—the post-Pericles Athens, an Athens that had passed the summit of its glory and was now on the decline. The Bible says of it at this period: "All the Athenians and strangers which were there spent their time in nothing else but either to tell or to hear some new thing."

No radios, no cables, no news dispatches; those Athenians must have been hard put in those days to scratch up something fresh every afternoon. Then Paul came. Here was something new. They crowded about him, amused, curious, interested. Taking him to the Aeropagus, they said: "May we know what this new doctrine, whereof thou speakest, is? For thou bringest certain strange things to our ears: we would know therefore what these things mean."

In other words, they invited a speech; and, nothing loath, Paul agreed. In fact, that was what he had come for. He probably stood up on a block or stone, and, being a bit nervous, as all good speakers are at the very outset, he may have given his hands a dry wash, and have cleared his throat before he began.

However, he did not altogether approve of the way they had worded their invitation; "New doctrines…strange things." That was poison. He must eradicate those ideas. They were fertile ground for the propagating of contradictory and clashing opinions. He did not wish to present his faith as something strange and alien. He wanted to tie it up to, liken it to, something they already believed. That would smother dissenting suggestions. But how? He thought a moment; hit upon a brilliant plan; he began his immortal address: "Ye men of Athens, I perceive that in all things ye are very superstitious."

Some translations read, "Ye are very religious." I think that is better, more accurate. They worshipped many gods; they were very religious. They were proud of it. He complimented them, pleased them. They began to warm toward him. One of the rules of the art of effective speaking is to support a statement by an illustration. He does just that:

"For, as I passed by, and beheld your devotions, I found an altar with this inscription, TO THE UNKNOWN GOD."

That proves, you see, that they were very religious. They were so afraid of slighting one of the deities that they had put up an altar to the unknown God, a sort of blanket insurance policy to provide against all unconscious slights and unintentional oversights. Paul, by mentioning this specific altar, indicated that he was not dealing in flattery; he showed that his remark was a genuine appreciation born of observation.

Now, here comes the consummate rightness of this opening: "Whom therefore ye ignorantly worship, Him declare I unto you."

"New doctrine…strange things?" Not a bit of it. He was there merely to explain a few truths about a God they were already worshipping without being conscious of it. Likening the things they did not believe, you see, to something they already passionately accepted—such was his superb technique.

He pronounced his doctrine of salvation and resurrection, quoted a few words from one of their own Greek poets; and he was done. Some of his hearers mocked, but others said, "We will hear thee again on this matter."

Our problem in making a talk to convince or impress others is just this: to plant the idea in their minds and to keep contradicting and opposing ideas from arising. He who is skilled in doing that has power in speaking and influencing others. Here is precisely where the rules in my book *How to Win Friends and Influence People* will be helpful.

Almost every day of your life you are talking to people

who differ from you on some subject under discussion. Aren't you constantly trying to win people to your way of thinking, at home, in the office, in social situations of all kinds? Is there room for improvement in your methods? How do you begin? By showing Lincoln's tact and Macmillan's? If so, you are a person of rare diplomacy and extraordinary discretion. It is well to remember Woodrow Wilson's words, "If you come to me and say, 'Let us sit down and take counsel together, and, if we differ from one another, understand why it is that we differ from one another, just what the points at issue are,' we will presently find that we are not so far apart after all, that the points on which we differ are few and the points on which we agree are many, and that if we only have the patience and the candor and the desire to get together, we will get together."

Points to Remember

1. The speech should reflect your sincerity.
2. Benefit from the 'Yes-Response' technique.
3. Friendly approach with the audience enables them to connect with you better.

19

INFLUENCING BY PERSUASION

"Nobody is more persuasive than a good listener."

More good and more ill have been effected by persuasion than by any other form of speech. It is an attempt to influence by means of appeal to some particular interest held important by the hearer. Its motive may be high or low, fair or unfair, honest or dishonest, calm or passionate, and hence its scope is unparalleled in public speaking.

This "instilment of conviction," to use Matthew Arnold's expression, is naturally a complex process in that it usually includes argumentation and often employs suggestion, as the next chapter will illustrate. In fact, there is little public speaking worthy of the name that is not in some part persuasive, for men rarely speak solely to alter men's opinions—the ulterior purpose is almost always action.

The nature of persuasion is not solely intellectual, but is largely emotional. It uses every principle of public speaking, and every "form of discourse," to use a rhetorician's expression, but argument supplemented by special appeal is its peculiar quality. This we may best see by examining the methods of persuasion.

THE METHODS OF PERSUASION

High-minded speakers often seek to move their hearers to action by an appeal to their highest motives, such as love of liberty.

The appeal to prejudice is effective—though not often, if ever, justifiable; yet so long as special pleading endures this sort of persuasion will be resorted to. Rudyard Kipling uses this method—as have many others on both sides—in discussing the great European war. Mingled with the appeal to prejudice, Mr. Kipling uses the appeal to self-interest; though not the highest, it is a powerful motive in all our lives. Notice how at the last the pleader sweeps on to the highest ground he can take. This is a notable example of progressive appeal, beginning with a low motive and ending with a high one in such a way as to carry all the force of prejudice yet gain all the value of patriotic fervor.

> Through no fault nor wish of ours we are at war with Germany, the power which owes its existence to three well-thought-out wars; the power which, for the last twenty years, has devoted itself to organizing and preparing for this war; the power which is now fighting to conquer the civilized world.
>
> For the last two generations the Germans in their books, lectures, speeches and schools have been carefully taught that nothing less than this world-conquest was the object of their preparations and their sacrifices. They have prepared carefully and sacrificed greatly.
>
> We must have men and men and men, if we, with our allies, are to check the onrush of organized barbarism.
>
> Have no illusions. We are dealing with a strong and magnificently equipped enemy, whose avowed aim is our complete destruction. The violation of Belgium, the attack

on France and the defense against Russia, are only steps by the way. The German's real objective, as she always has told us, is England, and England's wealth, trade and worldwide possessions.

If you assume, for an instant, that the attack will be successful, England will not be reduced, as some people say, to the rank of a second rate power, but we shall cease to exist as a nation. We shall become an outlying province of Germany, to be administered with that severity German safety and interest require.

We are against such a fate. We enter into a new life in which all the facts of war that we had put behind or forgotten for the last hundred years, have returned to the front and test us as they tested our fathers. It will be a long and a hard road, beset with difficulties and discouragements, but we tread it together and we will tread it together to the end.

Our petty social divisions and barriers have been swept away at the outset of our mighty struggle. All the interests of our life of six weeks ago are dead. We have but one interest now, and that touches the naked heart of every man in this island and in the empire.

If we are to win the right for ourselves and for freedom to exist on earth, every man must offer himself for that service and that sacrifice.

From these examples it will be seen that the particular way in which the speakers appealed to their hearers was by coming close home to their interests, and by themselves showing emotion—two very important principles which you must keep constantly in mind.

To accomplish the former requires a deep knowledge of

human motive in general and an understanding of the particular audience addressed. What are the motives that arouse men to action? Think of them earnestly, set them down on the tablets of your mind, study how to appeal to them worthily. Then, what motives would be likely to appeal to your hearers? What are their ideals and interests in life? A mistake in your estimate may cost you your case. To appeal to pride in appearance would make one set of men merely laugh—to try to arouse sympathy for the Jews in Palestine would be wasted effort among others. Study your audience, feel your way, and when you have once raised a spark, fan it into a flame by every honest resource you possess.

The larger your audience the more sure you are to find a universal basis of appeal. A small audience of bachelors will not grow excited over the importance of furniture insurance; most men can be roused to the defence of the freedom of the press.

Patent medicine advertisement usually begins by talking about your pains—they begin on your interests. If they first discussed the size and rating of their establishment, or the efficacy of their remedy, you would never read the ad. If they can make you think you have nervous troubles you will even plead for a remedy—they will not have to try to sell it.

The patent medicine men are pleading—asking you to invest your money in their commodity—yet they do not appear to be doing so. They get over on your side of the fence, and arouse a desire for their nostrums by appealing to your own interests.

Points to Remember

1. People are easy to influence when you appeal to their interest.
2. Persuasion as a form of public speech.
3. Study your audience to understand their interests and ideals.

20

HOW TO CRITICIZE—AND NOT BE HATED FOR IT

"Any fool can criticize, condemn, and complain but it takes character and self control to be understanding and forgiving."

Charles Schwab was passing through one of his steel mills one day at noon when he came across some of his employees smoking. Immediately above their heads was a sign that said No Smoking. Did Schwab point to the sign and say, "Can't you read?" Oh, no, not Schwab. He walked over to the men, handed each one a cigar, and said, "I'll appreciate it, boys, if you will smoke these on the outside." They knew that he knew that they had broken a rule—and they admired him because he said nothing about it and gave them a little present and made them feel important. Couldn't keep from loving a man like that, could you?

John Wanamaker used the same technique. Wanamaker used to make a tour of his great store in Philadelphia every day. Once he saw a customer waiting at a counter. No one was paying the slightest attention to her. The salespeople? Oh, they were in a huddle at the far end of the counter laughing and talking among themselves. Wanamaker didn't say a word.

Quietly slipping behind the counter, he waited on the woman himself and then handed the purchase to the salespeople to be wrapped as he went on his way.

Public officials are often criticized for not being accessible to their constituents. They are busy people, and the fault sometimes lies in overprotective assistants who don't want to overburden their bosses with too many visitors. Carl Langford, who had been mayor of Orlando, Florida, the home of Disney World, for many years, frequently admonished his staff to allow people to see him. He claimed he had an "open-door" policy; yet the citizens of his community were blocked by secretaries and administrators when they called.

Finally the mayor found the solution. He removed the door from his office! His aides got the message, and the mayor had a truly open administration from the day his door was symbolically thrown away.

Simply changing one three-letter word can often spell the difference between failure and success in changing people without giving offense or arousing resentment.

Many people begin their criticism with sincere praise followed by the word "but" and ending with a critical statement. For example, in trying to change a child's careless attitude toward studies, we might say, "We're really proud of you, Johnnie, for raising your grades this term. *But* if you had worked harder on your algebra, the results would have been better."

In this case, Johnnie might feel encouraged until he heard the word "but." He might then question the sincerity of the original praise. To him, the praise might seem only to be a contrived lead-in to a critical inference of failure. Credibility would be strained, and we probably would not achieve our objective of changing Johnnie's attitude toward his studies.

This could be easily overcome by changing the word "but"

to "and." "We're really proud of you, Johnnie, for raising your grades this term, *and* if you continue the same conscientious efforts next term, your algebra grade can be up with all the others."

Now, Johnnie would accept the praise because there was no follow-up of an inference of failure. We have called his attention to the behavior we wished to change indirectly, and the chances are he will try to live up to our expectations.

Calling attention indirectly to someone's mistakes works wonders with sensitive people who may resent bitterly any direct criticism. Marge Jacob of Woonsocket, Rhode Island, told one of our classes how she convinced some sloppy construction workers to clean up after themselves when they were building additions to her house.

For the first few days of the work, when Mrs. Jacob returned from her job, she noticed that the yard was strewn with the cut ends of lumber. She didn't want to antagonize the builders, because they did excellent work. So after the workers had gone home, she and her children picked up and neatly piled all the lumber debris in a corner. The following morning she called the foreman to one side and said, "I'm really pleased with the way the front lawn was left last night; it is nice and clean and does not offend the neighbors." From that day forward the workers picked up and piled the debris to one side, and the foreman came in each day seeking approval of the condition the lawn was left in after a day's work.

One of the major areas of controversy between members of the army reserves and their regular army trainers is haircuts. The reservists consider themselves civilians (which they are most of the time) and resent having to cut their hair short.

Master Sergeant Harley Kaiser of the 542nd USAR School addressed himself to this problem when he was working with a group of reserve non-commissioned officers. As an old-time regular-army master sergeant, he might have been expected to yell at his troops and threaten them. Instead he chose to make his point indirectly.

"Gentlemen," he started, "you are leaders. You will be most effective when you lead by example. You must be the example for your men to follow. You know what the army regulations say about haircuts. I am going to get my hair cut today, although it is still much shorter than some of yours. You look at yourself in the mirror, and if you feel you need a haircut to be a good example, we'll arrange time for you to visit the post barbershop."

The result was predictable. Several of the candidates did look in the mirror and went to the barbershop that afternoon and received "regulation" haircuts. Sergeant Kaiser commented the next morning that he already could see the development of leadership qualities in some of the members of the squad.

On March 8, 1887, the eloquent Henry Ward Beecher died. The following Sunday, Lyman Abbott was invited to speak in the pulpit left silent by Beecher's passing. Eager to do his best, he wrote, rewrote, and polished his sermon with the meticulous care of a Flaubert. Then he read it to his wife. It was poor—as most written speeches are. She might have said, if she had had less judgment, "Lyman, that is terrible. That'll never do. You'll put people to sleep. It reads like an encyclopedia. You ought to know better than that after all the years you have been preaching. For heaven's sake, why don't you talk like a human being? Why don't you act natural? You'll disgrace yourself if you ever read that stuff."

That's what she *might* have said. And, if she had, you know what would have happened. And she knew too. So, she merely remarked that it would make an excellent article for the *North American Review*. In other words, she praised it and at the same time subtly suggested that it wouldn't do as a speech. Lyman Abbott saw the point, tore up his carefully prepared manuscript, and preached without even using notes.

> **Points to Remember**
>
> 1. Modify your vocabulary to soften the blow of criticism.
> 2. Never directly address someone's error.
> 3. If you have to criticize once, praise thrice.

21

HOW TO CLOSE A TALK

*"There is only one excuse for a speaker's asking the
attention of his audience: he must have either
truth or entertainment for them."*

Would you like to know in what parts of your speech you are most likely to reveal your inexperience or your expertness, your inaptitude or your finesse? I'll tell you: in the opening and the closing. There is an old saying in the theatre, referring, of course, to actors, that goes like this: "By their entrances and their exits shall ye know them."

The beginning and the ending: They are the hardest things in almost any activity to manage adroitly. For example, at a social function aren't the most trying feats the graceful entrance and the graceful leave-taking? In a business interview, aren't the most difficult tasks the winning approach and the successful close?

The close is really the most strategic point in a speech; what one says last, the final words left ringing in the ears when one ceases—these are likely to be remembered longest. Beginners, however, seldom appreciate the importance of this coign of vantage. Their endings often leave much to be desired.

What are their most common errors? Let us discuss a few

and search for remedies.

First, there is the man who finishes with: "That is about all I have to say on the matter; so I guess I shall stop." That is not an ending. That is a mistake. That reeks of the amateur.

That is almost unpardonable. If that is all you have to say, why not round off your talk, and promptly take your seat and stop without talking about stopping. Do that, and the inference that that is all you have to say may, with safety and good taste, be left to the discernment of the audience.

Then there is the speaker who says all he has to say, but he does not know how to stop. I believe it was Josh Billings who advised people to take the bull by the tail instead of the horns, since it would be easier to let go. This speaker has the bull by the frontal extremities, and wants to part company with him, but try as hard as he will, he can't get near a friendly fence or tree. So he finally thrashes about in a circle, covering the same ground, repeating himself, leaving a bad impression…

The remedy? An ending has to be planned some time, doesn't it? Is it the part of wisdom to try to do it after you are facing an audience, while you are under the strain and stress of talking, while your mind must be intent on what you are saying? Or does common sense suggest the advisability of doing it quietly, calmly, beforehand?

Even such accomplished speakers as Webster, Bright, Gladstone, with their admirable command of the English language, felt it necessary to write down and all but memorize the exact words of their closings.

The beginner, if he follows in their footsteps, will seldom have cause to regret it. He ought to know very definitely with what ideas he is going to close. He ought to rehearse the ending several times, using not necessarily the same phraseology during each repetition, but putting the thoughts definitely into words.

An extemporaneous talk, during the process of delivery, sometimes has to be altered very materially; has to be cut and slashed to meet unforeseen developments, to harmonize with the reactions of one's hearers; so it is really wise to have two or three closings planned. If one does not fit, another may.

Some speakers never get to the end at all. Along in the middle of their journey, they begin to sputter and misfire like an engine when the petrol supply is about exhausted; after a few desperate lunges, they come to a complete standstill, a breakdown. They need, of course, better preparation, more practice—more petrol in the tank.

Many novices stop too abruptly. Their method of closing lacks smoothness, lacks finish. Properly speaking, they have no close; they merely cease suddenly, jerkily. The effect is unpleasant, amateurish. It is as if a friend in a social conversation were to break off brusquely and dart out of the room without a graceful leave-taking.

No less a speaker than Lincoln made that mistake in the original draft of his first inaugural. That speech was delivered at a tense time. The black storm clouds of dissension and hatred were already milling overhead. A few weeks later, the cyclone of blood and destruction burst upon the nation. Lincoln, addressing his closing words to the people of the South, had intended to end in this fashion:

> In your hands, my dissatisfied fellow-countrymen, and not in mine, is the momentous issue of the civil war. The government will not assail you. You can have no conflict without being yourselves the aggressors. You have no oath registered in heaven to destroy the government, while I have a most solemn one to preserve, protect and defend it. You can forbear the assault upon it. I cannot shrink from

the defence of it. With you and not with me is the solemn question of "Shall it be peace or a sword?"

He submitted his speech to Secretary Seward. Seward quite appropriately pointed out that the ending was too blunt, too abrupt, too provocative. So Seward himself tried his hand at a closing; in fact, he wrote two. Lincoln accepted one of them and used it, with slight modifications, in place of the last three sentences of the close he had originally prepared. The result was that his First Inaugural Address now lost its provocative abruptness and rose to a climax of friendliness, of sheer beauty and poetical eloquence:

> I am loth to close. We are not enemies but friends. We must not be enemies. Though passion may have strained, it must not break our bonds of affection. The mystic chords of memory, stretching from every battlefield and patriot's grave to every living heart and hearthstone all over this broad land, will swell the chorus of the Union when again touched, as surely they will be, by the better angel of our nature.

How can a beginner develop the proper *feeling* for the close of an address? By mechanical rules?

No. Like culture, it is too delicate for that. It must be a matter of sensing, almost of intuition. Unless a speaker can *feel* when it is done harmoniously, adroitly, how can he himself hope to do it?

However, this *feeling* can be cultivated; this expertness can be developed somewhat, by studying the ways in which accomplished speakers have achieved it. Here is an illustration, the close of an address by the then Prince of Wales before the Empire Club of Toronto:

> I am afraid, gentlemen, that I have departed from my reserve, and talked about myself a good deal too much. But I wanted to tell you, as the largest audience that I have been privileged to address in Canada, what I feel about my position and the responsibility which it entails. I can only assure you that I shall always endeavour to live up to that great responsibility and to be worthy of your trust.

A blind man listening to that talk would *feel* that it was ended. It isn't left dangling in the air like a loose rope. It isn't left ragged and jagged. It is rounded off, it is finished.

The famous Dr. Harry Emerson Fosdick spoke in the Geneva Cathedral of St. Pierre the Sunday after the opening of the sixth assembly of the League of Nations. He chose for his text: "All they that take the sword shall perish with the sword." Note the beautiful and lofty and powerful way in which he brought his sermon to a close:

> We cannot reconcile Jesus Christ and war—that is the essence of the matter. That is the challenge which today should stir the conscience of Christendom. War is the most colossal and ruinous social sin that afflicts mankind; it is utterly and irremediably unchristian; in its total method and effect it means everything that Jesus did not mean and it means nothing that he did mean; it is a more blatant denial of every Christian doctrine about God and man than all the theoretical atheists on earth ever could devise. It would be worthwhile, would it not, to see the Christian Church claim as her own this greatest moral issue of our time, to see her lift once more as in our fathers' days, a clear standard against the paganism of this present world and, refusing to hold

> her conscience at the beck and call of belligerent states, put the kingdom of God above nationalism and call the world to peace? That would not be the denial of patriotism but its apotheosis.
>
> Here today, as an American, under this high and hospitable roof, I cannot speak for my government, but both as an American and as a Christian I do speak for millions of my fellow citizens in wishing your great work, in which we believe, for which we pray, our absence from which we painfully regret, the eminent success which it deserves. We work in many ways for the same end—a world organized for peace. Never was an end better worth working for. The alternative is the most appalling catastrophe mankind has ever faced. Like gravitation in the physical realm, the law of the Lord in the moral realm bends for no man and no nation: "All they that take the sword shall perish with the sword."

But this collection of speech endings would not be complete without the majestic tones, the organ-like melody of the close of Lincoln's Second Inaugural. The late Earl Curzon of Keddleston, Chancellor of Oxford University, declared that this selection was "among the glories and treasures of mankind...the purest gold of human eloquence, nay, of eloquence almost divine":

> Fondly do we hope, fervently do we pray, that this mighty scourge of war may speedily pass away. Yet if God wills that it continue until all the wealth piled by the bondsman's two hundred and fifty years of unrequited toil shall be sunk, and until every drop of blood drawn with the lash shall be paid by another drawn with the sword, as was said three thousand years ago, so still it must be said

that "the judgments of the Lord are true and righteous altogether".

With malice toward none; with charity for all; with firmness in the right, as God gives us to see the right, let us strive on to finish the work we are in; to bind up the nation's wounds; to care for him who shall have borne the battle, and for his widow and his orphan—to do all which may achieve and cherish a just and lasting peace among ourselves, and with all nations.

You have just read, my dear reader, what is, in my opinion, the most beautiful speech ending ever delivered by the lips of mortal man… Do you agree with my estimate? Where, in all the range of speech literature, will you find more humanity, more sheer loveliness, more sympathy?

"Noble as was the Gettysburg Address," says William E. Barton in *Life of Abraham Lincoln*, "this rises to a still higher level of nobility… It is the greatest of the addresses of Abraham Lincoln and registers his intellectual and spiritual power at their highest altitude."

"This was like a sacred poem," wrote Carl Schurz. "No American President had ever spoken words like these to the American people. America had never had a president who had found such words in the depths of his heart."

But you are not going to deliver immortal pronouncements as President in Washington or as Prime Minister in Ottawa or Melbourne. Your problem, perhaps, will be how to close a simple talk before a group of businessmen. How shall you set about it? Let us search a bit. Let us see if we cannot uncover some fertile suggestions.

SUMMARIZE YOUR POINTS

Even in a short talk of three to five minutes, a speaker is very apt to cover so much ground that at the close the listeners are a little hazy about all his main points. However, few speakers realize that. They are misled into assuming that because these points are crystal clear in their own minds, they must be equally lucid to their hearers. Not at all. The speaker has been pondering over his ideas for some time. But his points are all new to the audience; they are flung at the audience like a handful of shot. Some may stick, but the most are liable to roll off in confusion. The hearers are liable, like Iago, to "remember a mass of things but nothing distinctly".

Some anonymous Irish politician is reported to have given this recipe for making a speech: "First, tell them that you are going to tell them, then tell them, then tell them that you have told them." Not bad, you know. In fact, it is often highly advisable to "tell them that you have told them". Briefly, of course, speedily—a mere outline, a summary.

Here is a good example. The speaker is a student of Mr. Bills' class in Public Speaking. He is also a traffic manager for railways:

> In short, gentlemen, our own backdoor yard experience with this block device, the experience in its use in the East, in the West, in the North—the sound operating principles underlying its operation, the actual demonstration in the money saved in one year in wreck prevention, move me most earnestly and unequivocally to recommend its immediate installation on our Southern branch.

You see what he has done? You can see it and feel it without having heard the rest of the talk. He has summed up in a few sentences, in sixty-two words, practically all the points he has made in the entire talk.

Don't you feel that a summary like that helps? If so, make that technique your own.

APPEAL FOR ACTION

The closing just quoted is an excellent illustration of the appeal-for-action ending. The speaker wanted something done: a block device installed on the Southern branch of his road. He based his appeal for it on the money it would save, on the wrecks it would prevent. The speaker wanted action, and he got it. This was not a mere practice talk. It was delivered before the board of directors of a certain railway, and it secured the installation of the block device for which it asked.

A TERSE, SINCERE COMPLIMENT

> The great state of Pennsylvania should lead the way in hastening the coming of the new day. Pennsylvania, the great producer of iron and steel, mother of the greatest railroad company in the world, third among our agricultural states—Pennsylvania is the keystone of our business arch. Never was the prospect before her greater, never was her opportunity for leadership more brilliant.

With these words, Charles Schwab closed his address before the Pennsylvania Society of New York. He left his hearers pleased, happy, optimistic. That is an admirable way to finish; but, in order to be effective, it must be sincere. No gross flattery. No extravagances. This kind of closing, if it does not ring true, will ring false, very false. And like a false coin, people will have none of it.

A HUMOROUS CLOSE

"Always leave them laughing," said George Cohan, "when you say goodbye." If you have the ability to do it, and the material, fine! But how? That, as Hamlet said, is the question. Each man must do it in his own individual way.

One would hardly expect Lloyd George to leave a gathering of Methodists laughing when he was talking to them on the ultra-solemn subject of John Wesley's Tomb, but note how cleverly he managed it. Note, also, how smoothly and beautifully the talk is rounded off:

> I am glad you have taken in hand the repair of his tomb. It should be honoured. He was a man who had a special abhorrence of any absence of neatness or cleanliness. He it was, I think, who said, "Let no one ever see a ragged Methodist." It is due to him that you never can see one. (Laughter.) It is a double unkindness to leave his tomb ragged. You remember what he said to a Derbyshire girl who ran to the door as he was passing and cried, "God bless you, Mr. Wesley". "Young woman," he answered, "your blessing would be of more value if your face and apron were cleaner." (Laughter.) That was his feeling about untidiness. Do not leave his grave untidy. If he passed along, that would hurt him more than anything. Do look after that. It is a memorable and sacred shrine. It is your trust. (Cheers.)

CLOSING WITH A POETICAL QUOTATION

Of all methods of ending, none are more acceptable, when well done, than humor or poetry. In fact, if you can get the proper verse of poetry for your closing, it is almost ideal. It will give the desired flavour. It will give dignity. It will give individuality. It will give beauty.

If you will go to the public library in your town and tell the librarian that you are preparing a talk on a certain subject and that you wish a poetical quotation to express this idea or that, she may be able to help you find something suitable in some reference volume such as Bartlett's book of quotations.

THE POWER OF A BIBLICAL QUOTATION

If you can quote a passage from Holy Writ to back up your speech, you are fortunate. A choice Biblical quotation often has a profound effect. The well-known financier, Frank Vanderlip, used this method in ending his address on the Allied Debts to the United States:

> If we insist to the letter upon our claim, our claim will in all probability never be met. If we insist upon it selfishly, we realize in hatreds but not in cash. If we are generous, and wisely generous, those claims can all be paid, and the good we do with them will mean more to us materially than anything we would conceivably be parting with. "For whosoever will save his life shall lose it, but whosoever shall lose his life for my sake and the Gospel's, the same shall save it."

THE CLIMAX

The climax is a popular way of ending. It is often difficult to manage and is not an ending for all speakers nor for all subjects. But when well done, it is excellent. It works up to a crest, a peak, getting stronger sentence by sentence.

Lincoln used the climax in preparing his notes for a lecture on Niagara Falls. Note how each comparison is stronger than the preceding, how he gets a cumulative effect by comparing its age to Columbus, Christ, Moses, Adam, and so on:

> It calls up the indefinite past. When Columbus first sought this continent—when Christ suffered on the cross—when Moses led Israel through the Red Sea—nay, even when Adam first came from the hands of his Maker; then, as now, Niagara was roaring here. The eyes of that species of extinct giants whose bones fill the mounds of America have gazed on Niagara, as ours do now. Contemporary with the first race of men, and older than the first man, Niagara is as strong and fresh today as ten thousand years ago. The Mammoth and Mastodon, so long dead that fragments of their monstrous bones alone testify that they ever lived, have gazed on Niagara—in that long, long time never still for a moment, never dried, never frozen, never slept, never rested.

WHEN THE TOE TOUCHES

Hunt, search, experiment until you get a good ending and a good beginning. Then get them close together.

The speaker who does not cut his talk to fit in with the prevailing mood of this hurried, rapid age will be unwelcome and, sometimes, positively disliked.

No less a saint than Saul of Tarsus sinned in this respect. He preached until a chap in the audience, "a young man named Eutychus", went to sleep and fell out of a window and all but broke his neck. Even then he may not have stopped talking.

Who knows? I remember a speaker, a doctor, standing up one night at a University Club. It had been a long banquet. Many speakers had already talked. It was two o'clock in the morning when his turn came. Had he been endowed with tact and fine feeling and discretion, he would have said half a dozen sentences and let us go home. But did he? No, not he. He launched into a forty-five minute tirade against vivisection. Long before he was halfway through his audience were wishing that he, like Eutychus, would fall out of a window and break something, anything, to silence him.

Mr. Lorimer, the editor of the *Saturday Evening Post*, told me that he always stopped a series of articles in the *Post* when they were at the height of their popularity, and people were clamouring for more. Why stop then? Why then of all times?

"Because," said Mr. Lorimer—and he ought to know—"the point of satiation is reached very soon after that peak of popularity."

The same wisdom will apply, and ought to be applied, to speaking. Stop while the audience is still eager to have you go on.

The greatest speech Christ ever delivered, the Sermon on the Mount, can be repeated in five minutes. Lincoln's Gettysburg address has only ten sentences. One can read the whole story of creation in Genesis in less time than it takes to peruse a murder story in the morning paper... Be brief! Be brief!

Dr. Johnson, Archdeacon of Nyasa, has written a book about the primitive peoples of Africa. He has lived among them, observed them, for forty-nine years. He relates that when a speaker talks too long at a village gathering or the Gwangwara, the audience silences him with shouts of "Imetosha! Imetosha!"—"Enough! Enough!"

Another tribe is said to permit a speaker to hold forth only so long as he can stand on one foot. When the toe of the lifted member touches the ground, *finito*. He has come to an end.

And the average white audience, even though they are more polite, more restrained, dislike long speeches as much as do those African negroes.

> So be warned by their lot,
> Which I know you will not,
> And learn about speaking from them.

Points to Remember

1. Know how to camouflage your inexperience in your speech.
2. The most essential thing is to plan your opening and closing statement.
3. Gain insight from established speakers.

22

STARTING TO COMMUNICATE

"Practice, practice, PRACTICE in speaking before an audience will tend to remove all fear of audiences, just as practice in swimming will lead to confidence and facility in the water. You must learn to speak by speaking."

Nothing could be easier than failing to communicate. Condescending, contradicting, berating, demeaning, treating other people as if "I am the boss, and you just work here"—until recently these were widely accepted forms of human interaction inside some of the largest and best-known companies in the world. "Barking rights" were thought to be a natural prerogative of executive positions, along with an office window and a two-hour lunch. Families, schools, and other organizations unfortunately followed suit.

For years loudness was equated with toughness. Stubbornness was equated with superior knowledge. Argumentativeness was equated with honesty. We should all—supervisor and employee, parent and child, teacher and student—be grateful those days are finally coming to an end.

More and more people, in businesses and elsewhere, are beginning to understand how important good communication really is. The ability to communicate well is what lights the fire in people. It's what turns great ideas into action. It's what makes all achievement possible.

Communicating well is not terribly complicated—not in theory, anyway. Communicating, after all, is something every one of us does every day in our personal lives. We've all been communicating since the early days of childhood. At least we think we have. But true communication, effective communication, is in fact relatively rare in the adult world.

There's no secret recipe for learning to communicate well, but there are some basic concepts that can be mastered with relative ease. Here are the first steps to successful communication.

Follow them and you will be on your way.

1. Make communication a top priority.
2. Be open to other people.
3. Create a receptive environment for communication.

No matter how busy you find yourself during the work day, *you absolutely must make time to communicate*. All the brilliant ideas in the world are worthless if you don't share them. Communication can be accomplished in many ways—in meetings, in face-to-face sessions with colleagues, just walking down the hall, or stopping at the water cooler, or spending half an hour in the company lunchroom. What's most important is that communicating never stop.

Communication doesn't have to happen in big conference rooms. Some of the best corporate communication occurs in seemingly informal ways.

The need for effective communication doesn't stop at the office door. It extends to the home, to the school, to the church, even to the halls of science. Any place where people meet with people, communication is key.

It used to be that research scientists could spend their

whole lives in the laboratory, singlemindedly searching for the truths of the natural order. But those days are gone. In today's competitive world, even scientists need to listen and talk.

"Many scientists don't know how to effectively communicate what they are doing," says Dr. Ronald M. Evans, an eminent research professor at the Salk Institute for Biological Studies. "They know what they are doing. They have a pretty good idea of why they're doing it. But they have difficulty putting that into perspective, transmitting the ideas outside the laboratory. It's a major limitation at many levels. To obtain funding, you have to convince people that you're doing something that's important."

The biggest mistake managers used to make—besides thinking that all wisdom flowed from them—was failing to understand that communication absolutely has to be a two-way street. You have to share your ideas with others and listen to theirs. That's step number two: *Be open to other people—above, below, and beside.*

If you can show your colleagues you are receptive to their ideas, they're more likely to be receptive to yours—and to keep you honestly informed about the things you need to know. Show that you care about the future of the organization and that you care as much about them. And don't limit those displays of concern to your coworkers. Communicate the same genuine caring to your customers and your clients too.

It's a basic fact about communicating with people: they won't say what they think—and won't listen receptively to what you say—unless a foundation of genuine trust and shared interest has been laid. You can't be insincere. How you really feel about communication, whether you're open or not, comes through loud and clear, no matter what you say. "You know right away if somebody is approachable or if they're not,"

Olympic gymnast Mary Lou Retton has said. "When you get that feeling, you can read a person by nonverbal communication and body language. You know when somebody is standing in the corner and saying, 'Hey, I don't want to be talked to.'"

How can you avoid sending that message? Be open, like people, and let them know you do. Follow Retton's advice: "Being down-to-earth and humble is extremely important. I just try to put people at ease. Everybody's the same. I think everybody is on a certain level, whether you are the CEO of a company or a salesperson. It's just a different job." That's what creating a receptive environment is all about: putting people at ease.

It used to be easier than it is today. Television announcer and former baseball great Joe Garagiola remembers how much one-on-one contact there used to be between the players and the fans: "When we used to come off the field and go to our homes after the games, we would ride the subways with the same fans who were in the stands a few hours earlier.

"It wasn't uncommon for one of the fans to say, 'Hey, Joe, why did you swing at that third strike? Why didn't you let it go?' Now there isn't the same personal connection between the fan and the players other than reading about whether or not he's signing a six- or a seven-million-dollar contract."

One last thing to remember: *Once people do take the risk of telling you what they think, don't punish them for their openness. Do nothing—absolutely nothing—to discourage them from taking the risk of communicating again.*

"If an employee makes a suggestion that I don't agree with, then I have to be very delicate about the way in which I tell them I don't agree," says Fred J. Sievert, chief financial officer of the New York Life Insurance Company. "I want to encourage them to come back to me the next time and make another suggestion. Now, I told some of the people on my staff that I may disagree with them ninety-nine times out of a hundred, but I want them to keep coming to me with their views. That's what they get paid for. The one time out of a hundred is going to be of value, and I'm not going to view them as any weaker because I disagree with them the other times."

One in a hundred. That may not sound so impressive, but great fortunes have been made on odds less certain than that. That's why listening and sharing ideas is so important.

The truth of the matter is that communication is both a skill and an art. It's a process worth thinking about and practicing more than most people do. It sometimes involves showing personal vulnerability by putting your ideas on the line. You're sharing with others and asking them to share with you. That's not always easy. It takes work and time. Techniques have to be acquired and practiced constantly. But take heart. Practice does make perfect, or very nearly so.

Kuo Chi-Zu is the chief prosecutor in Taipei, Taiwan, and a tremendously compelling public speaker. But he wasn't always so comfortable talking in front of a group. As a rising young prosecutor, Chi-Zu was always being invited to address local organizations. He said no to the Rotary. He said no to the Lions. He said no to Junior Achievement. He was so frightened of the prospect of appearing in public—as many people are—that he turned every invitation down.

"Even if I were just attending a meeting," he remembers, "I always selected the seat at the far corner. And I almost never said a single word."

He knew this fear was slowing the progress of his career—not to mention keeping him awake at night in fits of anxiety. He knew he had to get a grip on his communication problem.

Then one day Chi-Zu was invited to speak at his old high

school, and he recognized at once that this was his opportunity. He had, after all, made great effort over the years to maintain a strong relationship with the school and with its students and graduates. If there was any audience he could trust—and that would feel open to what he had to say—this was the one.

So he agreed to appear, and he prepared himself as well as he could. He chose a subject he knew a tremendous amount about and cared deeply for: his job as a prosecutor. He built the speech around real-life examples. He didn't memorize. He didn't write out the words. He just walked up to the front of the school auditorium and spoke as if he were addressing a room full of friends, which he was.

The speech was a great success. From the podium he could see the eyes in the audience riveted on him. He could hear the people laughing at his jokes. He could feel their warmth and support, and when he was finished speaking, the students rose to their feet for a robust standing ovation.

Chi-Zu learned some valuable lessons about communication that day: how communication takes a certain openness and a trusting environment, what dividends successful communication can pay. Chi-Zu didn't stop there. He became a favorite on the Taipei lecture circuit and was quickly catapulted into the chief prosecutor's job.

He was finally learning to communicate.

COMMUNICATION IS BUILT ON TRUSTING RELATIONSHIPS.

Points to Remember

1. Good ideas turn out to be great ideas through communication.
2. Communication is a two-way street between an employer and employee.
3. A nurturing environment is crucial for healthy communication.